SCORE & REHEARSAL PREPARATION

A Realistic Approach for Instrumental Conductors

SCORE & REHEARSAL PREPARATION

A Realistic Approach for Instrumental Conductors

GARY STITH

Published by
Meredith Music Publications
a division of G.W. Music, Inc.
4899 Lerch Creek Ct., Galesville, MD 20765
http://www.meredithmusic.com

Cover photo: © 2007 michels/spotlight-studio

International Standard Book Number: 978-1-57463-175-3
Cataloging-in-Publication Data is on file with the Library of Congress.
Library of Congress Control Number: 2011926357
Printed and bound in U.S.A.

This text is dedicated to my wife, Joyce, who is my best friend,
#1 supporter, and chosen partner for life.
Thank you for your encouragement and patience
as I have labored through this project.
I love you very much and will forever be thankful
that the Lord brought us together.

CONTENTS

FOREWORD

Gary Stith, former conductor of the Houghton College Symphonic Winds, has made a significant contribution to our profession with his newest publication, *Score and Rehearsal Preparation: A Realistic Approach for Instrumental Conductors*. In the preparation of both band and orchestra scores, it is imperative that a well-planned course of study be outlined and documented. Gary Stith's publication systematically addresses the myriad details that need to be addressed before the downbeat of the first rehearsal.

This comprehensive publication carefully outlines a thorough but time efficient process for score study which includes the analysis of compositional structure, seating recommendations, interpretation, preparation of the score itself and basic rehearsal strategies. The *Score and Rehearsal Preparation Worksheet* itself is a wonderfully useful template that sequentially organizes the score study process and is based upon his three important phases of score preparation. The text also contains an expanded appendix section which includes numerous examples of orchestra, concert band and wind ensemble seating arrangements, standard orchestra and band instrumentation, a comprehensive list of instrument abbreviations, percussion assignment charts, and a sample compositional flowchart that will prove to be very valuable to both aspiring and seasoned directors. In addition, the selective and in-depth bibliography provides numerous valuable resources that are sure to assist and accelerate every step of the score preparation process.

This text is a wonderful contribution to our profession and is an essential supplemental companion for university methods classes. It will also prove valuable for conductors teaching in today's public schools and universities, as well as at the professional level. Gary Stith has effectively filled the 'gap' in dealing with the complexities of score study and instrumental music. Thank you Gary for making this important publication available to our profession!

Edward S. Lisk
Clinician, Conductor, Author
Oswego, New York

Preface

In March of 1990, my Williamsville East High School Wind Ensemble was afforded the opportunity to assist clinician Frank L. Battisti in a conducting clinic at the New York State Band Directors Association Symposium held annually in Syracuse. That was also the year of publication of his highly acclaimed text *Guide to Score Study for the Wind Band Conductor* which he co-authored with another of the icons of our field, Robert Garofalo.

During the course of the hour-long clinic session, Battisti articulated a number of specific items that every conductor should know regarding each and every piece about to be programmed *prior* to the initial rehearsal. I found myself very much "convicted" that day and made a personal pledge to be more thorough in those critical beginning stages of my own score preparation.

Over the course of the next few weeks, I agonized over some of the assertions he had made. I was haunted by his charge that "public school conductors have entirely too much rehearsal time" and his implication that many often learn their scores *during* their overly abundant number of rehearsals. It was during that early spring that I began doing what any "type A/concrete sequential" personality like me usually feels compelled to do... I started to make a *list!* That initial checklist consisted of every detail that I vowed to address in the preparation of every score I would ever study, rehearse and/or conduct.

The *Score & Rehearsal Preparation Worksheet* and accompanying text that has evolved during the last two decades can be used with *every* piece you will ever prepare and then can be *maintained* so that much of the necessary study will be minimized each time the same piece is programmed in the future. It will prove immensely helpful to you in three ways:

1. It delineates the specific facts and details of which we as conductors need to be cognizant, as well as the critical determinations that must be made prior to the initial downbeat of the first rehearsal.
2. It provides a systematic and concise worksheet upon which many of these important facts and decisions can be maintained for future repeated performances.
3. It furnishes an exhaustive listing of printed sources where invaluable assistance can be obtained during the early stages of score and rehearsal preparation.

It is my sincere and prayerful desire that this new guide and resource may prove beneficial to undergraduate and graduate conducting students, as well as to the many of us who have devoted our careers to this labor of love.

Gary Stith
Houghton, New York

Acknowledgements

I will be forever indebted to Carl and ElizaBeth Irwin, Jason Decker, Connie VanSlyke, and Timothy Topolewsky who graciously and generously served as proofreaders throughout this project. Their candid but supportive suggestions have proven enormously helpful.

I am also sincerely grateful to my son, David, who drew the iceberg sketch, designed all of the seating charts and most of the appendices, and assisted me with a great deal of professional advice regarding the layout of the book. It has been an extra blessing to have my son working alongside me on this publication.

It's also imperative that my most recent instrumental conducting students be thanked for their loving input, as well as for their willingness to serve as "guinea pigs" during the final developmental stages of the *Score and Rehearsal Preparation Worksheet*. Those students include Rebekah Bartlett, Kylie Brown, Ernest Chamberlain, Ryan Clark, Stephen Cledgett, Laura Danneker, Mary Elisabeth Doan, Matthew Geeze, Amy Gribben, Sarah Harms, Daryl Harshbarger, Lauren Hempfing, Luke Klingensmith, Bridget Lyon, Robert Martin, Katie Pitts, Brett Ricci, Rachel Smith, Adam Stack, Melyssa Swett and Michele Walton.

A special acknowledgment is due to my former conducting student Jonathan Vogan, who willingly prepared the U. S. Air Force Band seating chart at the request of another of his mentors, Dr. Lowell Graham.

A sincere thanks is also extended to my colleague, Sun Mi Ro, who assisted with some of the musical examples and the flowchart.

Thank you to Oxford University Press for granting permission for the inclusion of the full score to *Flourish for Wind Band* by Ralph Vaughan Williams.

I also extend my appreciation to Houghton College for granting me a one semester sabbatical leave during the Fall of 2010, which enabled me to have the necessary time to complete most of this project.

Finally, I want to express gratitude to my son-on-law, Michael Merrill, who gave me the final much-needed "nudge" to embark on the writing of this text.

INTRODUCTION

Why is score study important for a conductor? What are the measurable benefits of meticulously studying, preparing and practicing each new piece PRIOR to stepping onto the podium for the first rehearsal? How important is score study and rehearsal preparation in comparison with baton technique? These are all legitimate questions that need to be addressed.

Why is score study important for a conductor? The primary purpose is so that the conductor can develop an internal rendering or mental image of every detail of the work from which to aspire that is true to the composer's intentions and compositional style, the historical period the piece represents, and is musically artistic. The score is filled with musical clues or hints that, when combined with knowledge and experience, will lead the conductor to a characteristic re-creation of the piece as it was intended by the composer. In addition, command of the specific aspects of the score and each individual instrumental or vocal part will dictate the needed physical skills and technique necessary for the conductor to visually portray the work and effectively rehearse and perform it.

What are the measurable benefits of meticulous study and preparation of each score? Analytical and methodical score study usually results in musically authentic and imaginative interpretations of the work being performed. In addition, making important determinations and addressing critical tasks in advance of the first reading by the ensemble saves precious rehearsal time and results in far more aesthetically pleasing rehearsals.

How important is score study and rehearsal preparation in comparison with baton technique? Imagine seeing an iceberg drifting in the north Atlantic or Pacific Ocean. Captains of sea vessels in those regions are very accustomed to seeing these large edifices of ice seemingly floating on top of the water and are all too careful to avoid a close encounter that could prove devastating to their ship. However, as awesome as that visible mountain of ice may appear, these captains are also aware that underneath the surface there lies a far larger portion of the ice that decidedly dwarfs the visible "tip of the iceberg."

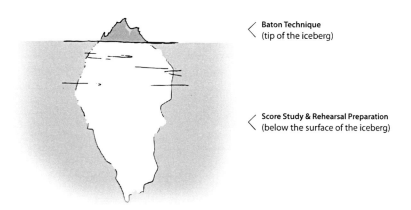

Baton Technique
(tip of the iceberg)

Score Study & Rehearsal Preparation
(below the surface of the iceberg)

Now imagine that the visible apex of the iceberg represents the amount of time devoted to conducting and rehearsing from the podium, and that the vast quantum of ice hanging beneath the surface represents the amount of advance score study and rehearsal preparation necessary to achieve an effective and artistic performance. Though audience members may only see the graceful motions of the conductor on concert night leading a sparkling and well-rehearsed performance, and the performers in the ensemble may only additionally notice the seasoned conductor leading and teaching during each of the preliminary rehearsals, what usually goes unnoticed is the enormous amount of study and preparation that was required by that conscientious conductor in order to achieve those effective rehearsals and the culminating aesthetically fulfilling performance.

The old saying holds true that during rehearsals and concert performances, every conductor should strive to have the "score in his head rather than his head in the score" and careful, methodical advance study is the best way to achieve this goal.

The intent of this text and the *Score and Rehearsal Preparation Worksheet* is to provide the conductor with a systematic procedure for studying each piece to be programmed prior to the scheduling of the first reading. It seeks to methodically include every necessary detail to be determined and helps to avoid FORGETTING any important considerations in your preparation. It is suggested that multiple copies of this blank worksheet be printed and all components be completed in advance and in their entirety for every piece you intend to program with your ensemble. It is further recommended that upon its completion, the conductor keep it inside the cover of his or her personal copy of the score so that whenever the same piece is programmed in the future, much of the preliminary study will already have been achieved. *This should prove to save the conductor many valuable hours of preparation.*

It should be made clear that in those subsequent performances of the work, much of the score study must begin again and fresh new interpretative ideas should always be considered. However, much of the initial study will have already been researched. Among those are basic biographical information about the composer, a glossary of musical terms used in the work, unusual instrumentation, seating determinations, corrected errors in score and parts, determination of percussion needs and distribution of parts, and a flowchart of the compositional structure of the work.

The Score and Rehearsal Preparation Worksheet is divided into the following three phases of study.

Phase I   Initial Overview of the Score
Phase II   Compositional Structure and Preparation of the Score
Phase III Interpretation and Preparation for the Initial Rehearsal

Let's get started!

SCORE & REHEARSAL PREPARATION WORKSHEET

(Title) _____

(Composer/Arranger) _____

❶ COMPOSER BACKGROUND

Dates and Places of Birth and Death _____
_____

Schools Attended _____
Former Teachers _____
Major Instrument(s) _____
Posts Held _____
_____

Awards & Achievements _____
_____
_____

General Compositional Style and Techniques _____
_____
_____

List of Significant Works

❷ Relevant Info Learned from Printed Text in Score _____
_____
_____
_____
_____
_____

❸ Duration of Piece _____ **❹ Date of Composition** _____

❺ Tempi _____ **❻ Level of Difficulty** _____

❼ Unusual Instrumentation *(list here)*

❽ Glossary of Italian, German or French Terms *(attached)*

❾ Numbered Measures in Score *(enter total here)* _____

❿ Recordings Studied *(list ensembles and conductors here)* _____
_____
_____

PHASE I

PHASE II

⓫ **Relevant Literature on the Work Studied** *(list title, author and periodical/texts)*

_____

_____

_____

_____

⓬ **Overall Form of Composition** _____ ⓭ **Keys**_____

⓮ **Flowchart of Entire Piece** *(attached)(✓)*___ ⓯ **Marked and Prepared Score** *(✓)*___

⓰ **Sang Through, Studied and Marked Each Individual Part in Score for Phrasing and Breath Marks** *(check off as completed)*

___ Piccolo	___ Cornets/Trumpets	___ 1st Violins
___ Flutes	___ Horns	___ 2nd Violins
___ Oboes	___ Trombones	___ Violas
___ English Horn	___ Euphonium/Baritones	___ Celli
___ Bassoons	___ Tubas	___ String Bass
___ Eb Clarinet	___ Harp	
___ Clarinets	___ Timpani	
___ Alto Clarinets	___ Snare Drum	___ Sopranos
___ Bass Clarinets	___ Mallet Percussion	___ Altos
___ Contra Bass/Alto	___ Remaining Percussion	___ Tenors
___ Saxophones	___ Piano	___ Basses

⓱ **Seating Recommendation** *(diagram here)*

PHASE III

⓲ **Percussion Parts Determined and Assigned** *(list here)*

⓳ **Solo/Soli/Section Parts Assigned** *(list here)*

⓴ **Errors Corrected in Score and Parts** *(check off when completed)* ___

㉑ **Anticipated Trouble Spots and Planned Reh. Strategies/Lesson Plan** *(attached)*

㉒ **Memorized Rehearsal Spots** *(list here)*

㉓ **Practiced Conducting in Front of Mirror** *(check off when secure)* ___

created by Gary Stith, Greatbatch School of Music, Houghton College
Houghton New York

PHASE I

INITIAL OVERVIEW OF THE SCORE

Phase I begins with the completion of the heading on the worksheet. Be sure to write or type the complete title of the musical composition, as well as the first, middle name or initial (if used) and last names of the composer (i.e. Johann Sebastian Bach, David R. Gillingham or in the provided example R. Vaughan Williams). If this piece is a transcription or an arrangement, be certain to include the complete name of the individual responsible for this edition. **It will also be important to list both the composer and arranger on your printed concert program.** This is both proper and respectful of the individual who spent many hours in the preparation of any special setting that your ensemble is about to prepare and perform.

Always be sure to spell composer and arranger names correctly. Composer names that are commonly misspelled include Aaron Copland (not Copeland), R. Vaughan Williams (not Vaughn), W. Francis McBeth (not MacBeth), and Percy Grainger (not Granger).

❶ Composer Background

The next part of Phase I is to complete the Composer Background. Although doing extensive research on the composer is always beneficial, every conductor from the collegiate or professional level to the elementary public school teacher/conductor must know, at least, some significant facts about the composer. This will help to provide the conductor with a solid basis from which to determine interpretive ideas about the piece, as well as enable the teacher/conductor the opportunity to serve as a music educator during rehearsals by providing some relevant historical information to the student or professional musicians. Be reminded that conductors are always, first and foremost, teachers no matter what the level of expertise of the musicians entrusted to them.

This section of the worksheet will require the conductor to seek out information regarding the following:

- composer's dates and places of birth and death
- colleges, universities, or conservatories attended
- former composition teachers who may have had an impact on the composer's compositional style
- major instrument(s)
- important posts held or institutions where he or she served on the faculty

- a few significant awards and/or achievements
- compositional style and/or techniques for which the composer is best known
- a brief list of significant works

In this latter category, seek to include works in all genres, not just band or orchestra. Band directors must, especially, seek to include more than just the composer's band pieces. *Remember that you are teaching "music" and not just "band" or "orchestra."*

Resources for this portion of your study are numerous. Be sure to see the Bibliography portion of this text that provides a series of possible sources. Online sources are also recommended, but **be careful that the provided information is accurate.** It is also recommended that you always seek more than one source. A "rule of thumb" is to check at least *three* and look for agreement amongst them. (Surprisingly, you will find inaccuracies and "differences of opinion" upon occasion, so be thorough in your "investigation.")

Please note that the space provided both here and in other places on the worksheet may be insufficient to accommodate all the information that you will have accumulated. Feel free to attach additional pages, when necessary.

➋ Relevant Facts Learned from Printed Info in Score

Next is to carefully and meticulously read and study every piece of preliminary information that is provided on the score cover, inside page and any additional pages provided. Much can be learned about the historical background and interpretation of each piece simply by reading every detail of this preliminary and supplemental information provided by the publisher.

To demonstrate this procedure, look at the included score to the *Flourish for Wind Band* by R. Vaughan Williams. Let's begin by looking at the cover. Items to notice include the following:

a) Full Score — This is not a condensed score. Full scores include each and every instrument part completely written out. It is probably a transposed score (all instrument parts transposed), but we won't know that for sure until we look at the music itself.

b) Composer Name — It's interesting that the publisher chose to use only his first initial. If you don't know this composer, it will be necessary to seek another source so that you can learn his first name. (Once again, note the spelling of his middle name.) As an aside, once you learn the first name of this composer, do a little extra "digging" to learn how to properly pronounce it. You may be surprised!

c) Title — *Flourish for Wind Band.* — What is a flourish? What is a wind band? Why isn't it called Flourish for Concert Band or Symphonic Band? This may have to be further researched.

d) Publisher — Oxford University Press (New York and Oxford). Is there any particular reason why this composer might have had his work published by a company based in NY and Oxford, England? Might this information hold a "clue" to the composer's nationality?

Next, let's turn the page and read the written information that appears on the inside cover. It starts by listing the instrumentation. All the needed instrument parts are listed in standard concert band or wind ensemble score order and include the number of parts provided in the published set. Upon occasion, this information may be included in the score, but usually not. This may prove very helpful as you seek to determine if you have sufficient players to perform this work with all parts covered.

Also notice the instruments listed in "square brackets." The paragraph above explains that these are "editorial additions to augment the score for U.S.A. wind band orchestration." This seems to "hint" that the piece might have been originally composed for a band in a different country. Make a note that you may have to look elsewhere to learn in what country this piece may have been premiered. These editorial additions include E flat Alto Clarinet, B flat Bass Clarinet, E flat Contra Alto and B flat Contrabass Clarinets, E flat Alto Saxophone II, E flat Baritone Saxophone, B flat Cornet III, Baritone Treble Clef, and String Bass.

The asterisks refer to the fact that the publisher chose not to show the Contrabass Clarinet or the String Bass parts in the score. This implies that these parts are probably doubled in some other parts. Where might that be?

Notice the (ad lib) printed after the Timpani listing. Be sure to look this term up in your music dictionary to determine exactly what this means.

You may also notice some unusual listings under the "Instrumentation." We will come back to these when we come to the **Unusual Instrumentation** portion of the worksheet.

Below the instrumentation, the publisher includes the duration of the piece. This will prove helpful as you determine your complete program for the concert on which you plan to include this work. You may skip down to ❸ **Duration of Piece** and enter this important information now. Please note that indicating the duration or length of a piece is not a common practice inside a score, but a small "bonus" when provided.

In addition to writing the duration of the piece on blank #4, it is also strongly recommended that you add this important piece of information at the top of the score or cover page where easily observable. Note that this figure may vary somewhat from that occasionally provided by the publisher or composer based upon your own desired tempi, as well as your intended rate of ritardandos or accelerandos. Your tempi may also be slightly impacted by the performance ability of the musicians in your ensemble.

The final paragraph indicates more valuable information. "An adaptation, by Roy Douglas, for orchestral wind is on hire." This means that a setting for reduced instrumentation (probably for orchestral wind and percussion section) is available on rental (hire). Even the publisher's choice of words such as "hire" seems to continue to "hint" that this work originated somewhere other than the U.S.A.

The final sentence reads "This work was composed as an Overture to the Pageant *Music and the People* and was first performed in the Royal Albert Hall, London, on 1 April 1939." Now we have learned that this was written as an opening to a pageant of some sort and premiered at the famous Royal Albert Hall in London (England). Now the choice of words we've been discovering begins to make sense. Is the composer British? Does the earlier reference to "U.S.A. wind band orchestration" imply that bands in England are comprised somewhat differently?

Finally, note that the exact date of this piece's first performance is provided. At this time, skip down to ❹ **Date of Composition** and enter 1939 as the probable date of its completion. Though it's possible that the composer actually completed the work prior to that date, further research would be necessary to determine that fact.

Before studying the printed music itself, be sure to turn to the back of the score to make sure that no additional information has been provided. Upon occasion this may be the case, but rather rarely. (An exception is the Fennell edition of Grainger's *Lincolnshire Posy* in which pages of additional information are provided at the back of the score.) However, this publisher has provided some very valuable information about this piece that may have been lost had the conductor not taken the time to carefully read it. Valuable rehearsal preparation time will have been saved due to this initial study of the printed text in the conductor's score.

Now, at last, it's time to look at the music itself. Look over the first page. Important information that you will learn includes the following:

a) Opening time signature (3/4)
b) Looking down at the various key signatures, it's apparent that this is, indeed, a transposed score.
c) The parts are listed in a generally accepted concert band score order (woodwinds at the top, brass in the middle, percussion at the bottom). The only differences you may notice are that the bassoon is listed after the bass clarinet and the horns are listed above the cornets and trumpets. Is it possible that this is more closely tied to the order found in an orchestral score?
d) Opening dynamic is *ff*.
e) Opening tempo is "maestoso" or majestic.
f) Take note of the composer's use of the tenor clef in the trombone part. If you were planning to program this piece with your public school band, your student trombonists may need to become familiar with this clef.
g) Notice also that the date of publication listed at the bottom reads "1972." Apparently this piece was not published until thirty-three years after its premiere.
h) Notice also that the piece opens with all brass and no woodwinds or percussion.

Turn the pages to obtain an overview of the piece. Among the important information you discover will include:

a) Woodwinds and percussion enter around letter A.
b) Key change one measure before B.
c) Dynamic level drops to *p* at B and seems to become more legato in style.
d) At letter C, the dynamic rises back to *ff*.
e) There is another key change in the 5th measure of C.
f) In the 10th measure of C, the scoring is again reduced to brass only.
g) At around D, the woodwinds and percussion rejoin.
h) The piece ends with a fermata.

❺ Tempi

Now let's go back and continue gathering data on the worksheet. As you go through the pages of this brief score, the only tempo marking seems to be the initial "maestoso." Write that term on the blank and look up the range of acceptable metronome markings for which this Italian word generally refers. This is a rather general term so there will be a range of tempi from which you will have to make an artistic determination.

In general, always list the principal tempi markings in chronological order on blank #5 (i.e. Maestoso — Andante — Allegro — Vivo *or* quarter note = 92, 72, 60, 88, 120). If only Italian tempo markings are provided by the composer, you will need to determine and provide your desired metronome markings next to those Italian terms prior to the first rehearsal. These should be printed clearly in your score.

❻ Level of Difficulty

As you seek to balance your program and/or seek to select music that is appropriate for the level of your students' ability, indicating the approximate level of difficulty will prove helpful. There are various sources from which you may find some indication in this regard.

a) Publishers of educational music often provide a guide on their scores, on the outer sleeve into which the score and parts are sold, or in their catalogues.
b) State music educator compilations and manuals often provide listings of quality music categorized by level of difficulty.
c) Other such lists also exist and can be found in the bibliography of this text.

If the piece for which you are considering does not appear on any such list, then it's probable level of difficulty will become apparent as you begin to study the individual parts.

❼ Unusual Instrumentation

Appendix A includes the standard instrumentation for both symphony orchestra and concert band/wind ensemble. Compare the appropriate page with the instrumentation listed in your score.

Items of which to take special note in **concert band/symphonic wind ensemble** pieces include the following:

a) Number of different Piccolo parts (None or one is standard, but exceptions do exist.

b) Number of different Flute parts (Two is standard)

c) Number of different Oboe parts (Two is standard)

d) Number of different Bassoon parts (Two is standard)

e) Contrabassoon parts

f) English Horn part

g) Eb Clarinet part (Many conductors choose to exclude the Eb Clarinet part in performance because of the frequent difficulty it presents in regard to achieving desirable ensemble blend and pitch. If it is determined that it is completely doubled in the 1st Clarinet or other part, you may elect not to use it. However, if it has distinctive solos, you may need to cover this important part.)

h) Number of Clarinet parts (Three is the standard, but this may vary upon occasion.)

i) Alto Clarinet part and its apparent usefulness. (Few ensembles use alto clarinets any more due to their usual poor tone quality and because they generally simply double another standard part. You will need to decide if it will be necessary to cover this part.)

j) ContraAlto or ContraBass Clarinet parts

k) Soprano Saxophone is not standard in wind bands. However, Percy Grainger used it quite frequently in his works for band.

l) Division of Cornets and Trumpets (This varies significantly from piece to piece in works for band. Taking note of this will enable you to assign parts in such a way as to achieve the desired balance within the section.)

m) Number of Horn parts (2 or 4). Also check to see if the parts are written for the standard F horns or, if a somewhat dated piece, Eb horns. In the latter case, you may need to have those parts transposed in advance of the 1st rehearsal.

n) Trombones (2 or 3 including a possible Bass Trombone part)

o) Euphoniums/Baritones. (If you use a Treble Clef baritone part for a recently "converted" trumpet player, make sure that such a part exists. Otherwise, you will need to write out a transposed part.)

p) Non-standard Percussion parts — These might include vibraphone, crotales, brake drums, tenor drum, bell tree, thunder sheet and so forth.

This will be very important to note so that you purchase or borrow the needed instruments *prior* to the first rehearsal.

q) Piano
r) Harp
s) String Bass
t) Celeste
u) Added antiphonal brass

Symphony orchestra instrumentation may vary significantly due to the evolution of its instrumentation through the centuries. In addition, you will need to take special note of pieces written specifically for string orchestra as opposed to full orchestra.

Items for which to take special note in an orchestral score include the following:

a) Piccolo (First used by Beethoven)
b) Flutes, Oboes, Bassoons, Clarinets, Trumpets, Horns, Trombones (Number depends upon the era in which the piece was written and/or the specific needs of the composer)
c) Bass clarinet
d) Saxophone (Rarely used, but there are some exceptions)
e) Euphonium (Rarely used, but there are some exceptions)
f) Tuba (Used infrequently enough that you will need to take note)
g) Non-standard Percussion parts (see (P) above)
h) Piano
i) Harp (Used more frequently than in band)
j) Celeste
k) Organ
l) Added antiphonal brass

❽ Glossary of Italian or German Terms

It will always be necessary to look up any musical terms found in the score for which you are unfamiliar. You should purchase a musical term dictionary for your use. You will find some specific recommendations in the bibliography.

For your initial score study project, it is strongly recommended that you make a complete list of every musical term found anywhere in the piece, including all expression and dynamic markings (i.e. *pp*, *mf*, *ff*, etc.). It is not unusual to discover that the definitions to which you have become accustomed may be somewhat incomplete or even incorrect. Make a separate alphabetical listing of each term found in the work and be sure to seek out at least three different sources.

Many seasoned and respected public speakers are often heard giving a definition of a term for which they have sought multiple definitions. This practice adds to our comprehension of each term and may help in explaining your interpretation of the term and related passage to the musicians in your ensemble.

It should also be noted that composers such as Percy Grainger used only terms and expressions in English. A glossary of "Graingerisms" is also recommended when studying his works because his use of terms is so unique.

Vaughan Williams makes use of such terms sparingly in his "Flourish for Wind Band," but a sample glossary can be found in Appendix B.

❾ Numbered Measures in Score

It is a recommended practice that the conductor take the time to number every measure in each score to be prepared. This simply means writing (in pencil) the number of each measure beginning with measure "1" at the top or bottom of the score from the beginning to the end. In multi-movement works, remember to number each movement individually, beginning with number "1." There are two principal reasons for this recommended practice:

1. When you begin reading chapters and/or articles about each piece you are studying, you will find that the authors often refer to specific passages in the music by measure number, and not necessarily by rehearsal letter. The simple reason is that this is faster and makes it easier and quicker for the reader to "pinpoint" the specific measure being discussed. (i.e. "measure 63" as opposed to "the 19th measure of B") When you begin item 11 in phase II, the merit of this practice will immediately become apparent.
2. When taking your ensemble to an adjudicated festival, this practice of numbering the measures in each of the scores presented to the adjudicators is often *required*. It makes their job much easier as they need to quickly refer to specific measures in their performance analysis while your ensemble is performing.

Some conductors require that all the musicians in their ensembles number the measures in their own parts to further save rehearsal time. The conductor will then refer to these measure numbers instead of rehearsal letters in rehearsal. This practice minimizes confusion among the ensemble members and reduces the number of times when some may find themselves starting in the wrong measure.

With relatively recent publications, some notation software includes the numbering of at least the first measure of each line of music. When this is the case, this somewhat time-consuming chore can be avoided or at least minimized.

It should be mentioned here that the numbering of measures can be done without much concentration. In most cases, it can be completed while watching television, riding on some form of public transportation, or even while sitting in the waiting room at the doctor's office!

On the blank next to "Numbered Measures in Score," it is suggested that the total number (that of the last measure of the piece or movement) be listed.

⑩ Recordings Studied

Here lies one of the most controversial issues in the systematic process of score study. Opinions vary significantly on this topic, but most are in agreement as follows:

a) Preparing to conduct a score by playing it at the piano is almost always preferred, if the conductor has sufficient piano skills. This allows one to formulate his or her own interpretation from a "clear mental slate" without being influenced by someone else's interpretation, no matter how reputable that individual may be. Remember that music is an art form and an informed interpretation should be somewhat personal. Simply copying or mimicking the interpretation of a noteworthy conductor is no longer art and reduces music making to an impersonal, exacting formula.

b) When time is very limited and it seemingly becomes advantageous to include the listening to a few recordings in your score preparation, use them very sparingly and attempt to find several. In this way, you will not be dramatically influenced by only one interpretation.

c) If seeking out recordings, be sure to limit your listening to those by reputable conductors and ensembles. Recordings on which the ensemble is conducted by the composer may prove especially valuable as you seek to ascertain his or her intended interpretation. However, finding random recordings of questionable merit on the internet and elsewhere can prove harmful to your score study and the subsequent desired artistic performance.

d) Never devote conducting practice time to "following" a recording. Once again, when doing this, you are following and not leading. Your dependence upon that recording will become instantly apparent the moment you begin rehearsing the piece in front of a "live" ensemble.

The use of recordings vary from conductor to conductor. Some prefer not to use them at all until, perhaps, after the performance of the piece. In this way, the conductor can compare genuine unbiased interpretations "after the fact" which may have some impact on a later programming of the work.

Personally, I choose to refer to several recordings in the very early stages of score preparation to become marginally familiar with the work, *and then put them away as the real score study begins.*

If you choose to refer to some fine recordings in the earliest stage of your score study, list them on the blanks provided on the worksheet. Listings should appear similar to the following:

Bernstein — NY Philharmonic
Tilson Thomas — San Francisco Symphony
Van Karajan — Berlin Philharmonic
                    or
Fennell — Eastman Wind Ensemble
Gabriel — U. S. Air Force Band
Corporon — North Texas Wind Symphony

You have now successfully completed the *Initial Overview of the Score.* Now on to Phase II!

FULL SCORE

R. Vaughan Williams

FLOURISH
FOR WIND BAND

OXFORD UNIVERSITY PRESS
NEW YORK AND OXFORD

Instrumentation:

Instruments in square brackets are editorial additions to augment the score for U.S.A. wind band orchestration. In the score, normal-sized notes show the composer's original; small notes are editorial additions.

1 Full Score	1 [E flat Baritone Saxophone]
5 Concert Flute	3 B flat Cornet I
1 Oboe	3 B flat Cornet II
1 Bassoon	3 [B flat Cornet III]
1 E flat Clarinet	2 B flat Trumpets I & II
3 B flat Solo Clarinet	2 F Horns I & II
3 B flat Ripieno Clarinet (I)	2 F Horns III & IV
3 B flat Clarinet II	2 Trombones I & II
3 B flat Clarinet III	1 Trombone III (Bass Trombone)
1 [E flat Alto Clarinet]	3 Euphonium (Baritone Bass Clef):
1 [B flat Bass Clarinet]	and [Baritone Treble Clef]
1 [E flat Contra Alto Clarinet;	5 Bass (Tuba)
and B flat Contrabass Clarinet]*	1 [String Bass] **
1 E flat Alto Saxophone (I)	1 Timpani (*ad lib.*)
1 [E flat Alto Saxophone II]	3 Percussion: Side Drum
1 B flat Tenor Saxophone	Bass Drum
	Cymbals

* Not shown in score—doubling Bass Clarinet
**Not shown in score—doubling Basses

Duration 1½ minutes
An adaptation, by Roy Douglas, for orchestral wind is on hire.
This work was composed as an Overture to the Pageant *Music and the People* and was first performed in the Royal Albert Hall, London, on 1 April 1939.

FLOURISH FOR WIND BAND

R. VAUGHAN WILLIAMS

Printed in U. S. A.

OXFORD UNIVERSITY PRESS, MUSIC DEPARTMENT

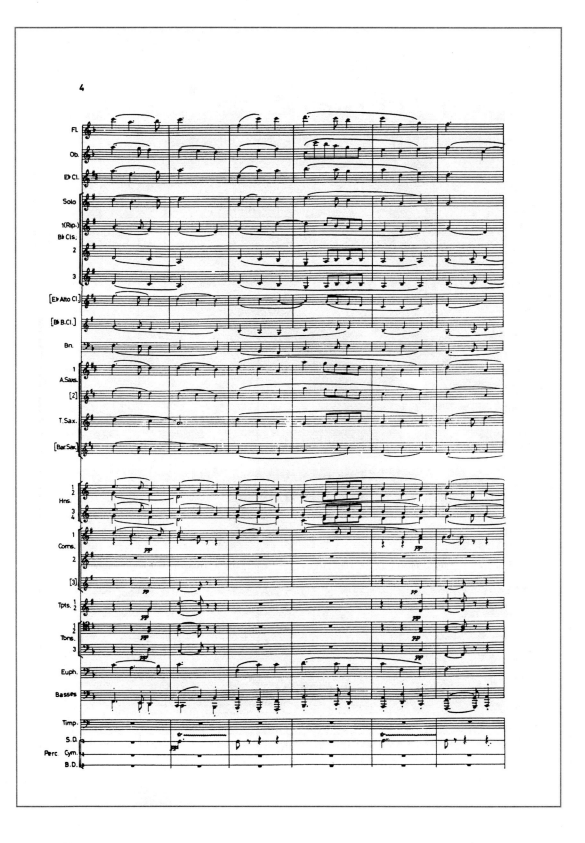

ISBN 0 19 389855 3

OXFORD UNIVERSITY PRESS

PHASE II

COMPOSITIONAL STRUCTURE AND PREPARATION OF THE SCORE

n this phase of score preparation, we will begin a more detailed analysis of the piece and embark on preparing the score for rehearsal.

⓫ Relevant Literature on the Work Studied (List title, author, & periodicals/texts)

As the old adage goes, "Why reinvent the wheel?" In other words, if some study or research has already been completed and/or published regarding the piece you are about to program, it makes perfect sense to save yourself some time and seek out those sources. Helpful information that might be gleaned from such research may include the following:

a) impetus for the composition of the work (the occasion or commission that prompted the creation of this piece of music)
b) date of its completion (which may vary from the copyright date)
c) date, ensemble and conductor of its premiere performance
d) additional and relevant composer biographical information
e) compositional form or structure
f) specific performance challenges within the piece
g) suggestions for interpretation and phrasing
h) recommended rehearsal strategies
i) suggestions for advantageous ensemble seating when performing and rehearsing this piece
j) listing of errata (errors) found in the published or existing score and parts
k) sources where additional information might be obtained
l) discography (listing of available recordings)

As useful information is garnered from each printed or online source, record your findings directly onto the pages of your full score and/or on the appropriate sections of your *Score & Rehearsal Preparation Worksheet*. In the case of recommended rehearsal strategies or seating suggestions, you may find it necessary to attach an extra page or two to your worksheet upon which you may write or diagram this valuable information. The major sections of the overall compositional form and themes should be labeled in pencil in your score, probably well above the top staff where it will be readily readable and out of the way of other important score markings.

The Selective Bibliography found in the back of this text includes a comprehensive list of resources that are grouped by the specific *phase* (I, II, or III) of score preparation. In addition, after each listing, you will find a series of numbers in parentheses (i.e. 1, 3, 6, 8, 11). These numbers correspond with those found on the *Worksheet* and indicate specific topical information that may be gleaned from that particular source. In addition, a constantly renewed listing can be found on the garystith.blogspot.com internet site. Be sure to refer to it in addition to the selective pages found in this text.

Searching for other relevant sites on the internet can also prove beneficial. However, remember that inaccuracies may appear from time to time so be sure to seek out reliable sites and *multiple* sources before accepting a piece of information (whether in print or online) as the "gospel truth."

To gain access to possible articles in significant periodicals, go to the corresponding website. Among others, *The Instrumentalist* has included enormously beneficial essays about many landmark instrumental works which have been authored by such conductors and composers as Frederick Fennell, Barry Kopetz, Karel Husa, W. Francis McBeth and others. If you are a subscriber to that professional journal, you may go online to their website, type in your *user name* and *password,* and then proceed to see what relevant articles may exist to assist you. If not a subscriber, please know that college and university libraries often house the complete set of these valuable magazines for your use. It should also be noted that the *Conductors Anthology Vol. II,* published by *The Instrumentalist*, contains all such articles dating up to 1993.

In regard to *Flourish for Wind Band*, "digging" into the selective bibliography and periodical archives will uncover a number of beneficial resources including the following:

Cannava, Edward. "Band Classics Revisited." *The Instrumentalist* 71 (May 1995).

Miles, Richard, compiler and editor. "'Flourish for Wind Band' Ralph Vaughan Williams," *Teaching Music through Performance in Band, Vol.* I. Chicago: GIA Publications, 1997 .

Stone, Stuart. "The Flowing Lines of Flourish for Wind Band." *The Instrumentalist* 28 (June 1999).

Mitchell, Jon Ceander, *Ralph Vaughan Williams' Wind Works.* Galesville, MD: Meredith Music Publications, 2008.

Randel, Don Michael, *The Harvard Dictionary of Music.* Cambridge, MA: The Belknap Press of Harvard University Press, 2003.

Careful study of these resources prior to the first rehearsal will significantly accelerate and enhance your score and rehearsal preparation of the work, as well as provide you with its somewhat historical significance. In addition, implementation of some of the performance suggestions and rehearsal strategies found in some of these publications will surely prove to make your practice sessions run more efficiently resulting in a more polished and artistic performance.

If you are among the large majority of individuals in the world who are either visual or kinesthetic (hands on) learners, you probably synthesize bodies of information best by "visualizing" and/or "doing" something physical. Taking notes and/or marking your score accordingly are highly recommended to those of you who fit into this category. It is suggested that you do the following with each piece of important information that you glean from your "investigative" study:

1. Add additional and relevant biographical information to the *Score & Rehearsal Preparation Worksheet* in section #1 (**Composer Background**).
2. Write the **Date of Composition** on blank #3 AND, in parenthesis, on the score itself next to the title (i.e. *First Suite in Eb* [1909]). In the unfortunate event that your score and its completed worksheet ever get separated, that critical information will still be readily available to you.
3. Take careful notes of all other suggestions that may prove beneficial to you and the musicians entrusted to your leadership. Remember that the reason for your "investigative legwork" is to significantly enhance your ability to teach, rehearse and conduct this piece. *The musicians sitting before you, whether elementary school students or mature professionals, deserve your very BEST.*

⑫ Overall Form of Composition

Knowledge of the themes and compositional structure are critical for the conductor to understand. This important information may have significance in relation to your overall comprehension and interpretation of the piece, as well as prove helpful in creating some effective rehearsal strategies. Determining that form and locating those important themes and compositional techniques will require the conductor to spend some time studying and analyzing the work. You may find some guidance as you read various articles, but *beware that you may find legitimate differences of opinion*. It is best to do your own formal analysis first, and then check your findings with those of some other authorities. Similar to doing detective work, approaching score analysis in this order is also more exciting and enlightening!

If you determine that the piece or movement fits into a rather standard compositional form or structure, write the name of that structure on blank #12. Such forms might include sonata allegro, rondo, ternary ABA or ABC, binary, strophic, as well as many others. Then go back to your score and write the principal sections of that formal structure over the appropriate measures at the top of the corresponding pages. For example, if you determine the form of a movement or piece to be sonata allegro, you will write the words "Exposition," "Development" and "Recapitulation" over the exact spot in the music where each appropriate section begins. If the piece is in rondo form, you will write "A Section," "B Section," "A Section," "C Section," "A Section," etc. at the top of the score over the measures where each of those particular sections begin.

In addition, be sure to label each of the important themes (A Theme, B Theme, etc.) and compositional techniques as they are introduced (Fugue Section, Augmentation, Diminution, etc). Remember that this work should always be done in pencil so that you can erase and make changes or corrections whenever necessary.

The Vaughan Williams score opens in Bb Major with the horns, trombones, cornets and trumpets playing a rather noble or dignified sounding theme in imitation style at the *ff* dynamic level. Characteristic in nature of a "flourish" or fanfare, this is probably either the introduction of the work or the A theme. Let's continue to examine the piece before making that determination.

At letter A (measure 11), all the woodwinds, euphoniums, tubas and percussion join the brass in a glorious statement of a theme, remaining at the *ff* dynamic level. **Is this a new theme or simply the second phrase of the initial one?**

At letter B (measure 20), the key changes to F Major and we are introduced to a more legato and harmonically luscious theme. The dynamic level has, rather suddenly, dropped to *p*. The new smooth, connected and lyrical sounding style of this theme seems entirely different from the majestic one at the opening of the work. **Could this be a new structural section?** The melodic material is also different from the opening so it's clearly a new theme. Your choices thus far are as follows:

a) Measures 1–19 is the introduction, and letter B begins the A theme
b) Measures 1–10 is an introduction, 11–19 is the A theme, and letter B begins the B theme
c) There is no introduction, measures 1–19 is the A theme and this softer section is the B theme

Before making a determination, let's see what comes next.

At the fifth measure of letter C (measure 40), the key changes back to the original key of Bb, and at measure 45, we find the return of the opening majestic theme, once again played by the horns, cornets, trumpets, and trombones. All the remaining instruments in the ensemble join again at letter D (measure 54) and the brief work concludes triumphantly nine measures later at the *ff* dynamic level. Either the composer chose to close with the introduction (which is rather unusual) or concludes with the return of the initial A section.

Hence, our formal structure options seem to be:

> **Intro. — A section — Intro.**
>   OR
> **Intro. — A section — B section — Intro. — A section**
>   OR
> **A section — B section — A section (ABA or ternary)**

Which makes more sense? If you said ABA, in all probability, you are correct. However, when you read some of the printed literature above about this piece by two very knowledgeable authors, you will discover a difference of opinion! You must make your own well-informed decision.

If you have concluded that this is ternary form, write ABA on blank #12 (***Overall Form of Composition***) and then print the beginning of each of the major sections (A, B, A) in pencil over the appropriate measures at the very top of your score. At the bottom of your score, indicate the key centers appropriately (Bb, F, Bb). You may also wish to "name" each of the themes such as:

A = majestic, dignified or noble theme
B = flowing or lyrical theme

Naming each of these appropriately may prove helpful during rehearsals as you seek to impart to the musicians your preferred interpretation of them.

This is also an opportunity for you to identify any compositional techniques and/or textures prominent in the piece. The opening section features an imitative style, which is reminiscent of the polyphonic, or even antiphonal, texture used in the Renaissance era. Beginning at the tutti section (where everyone is playing) at measure 11, the style changes to a more homophonic texture with a solitary theme supported harmonically. The polyphonic texture returns at measure 45 and the piece proceeds to a homophonic tutti from measure 54 to its climactic conclusion.

⓭ Keys

On this blank, simply list the major key centers in chronological order, or as they appear in the piece. Though you have just identified those keys at the bottom of the appropriate measures in your full score, this exercise will simply serve as a mental reminder of their sequence.

At this juncture, you should also ask yourself if Vaughan Williams' choice of modulations from Bb — F — Bb are logical or unusual. **Is it common to modulate to the dominant? Is it unusual to start and end in the same key?** Your background in basic theory and music history should help you answer these questions.

Another reason that the recording of key centers on your *Score & Rehearsal Preparation Worksheet* can prove valuable is to remind you to avoid programming too many pieces in one key on the same concert. I humbly speak from experience in this regard. In one of my first years of teaching, I accidentally programmed an entire middle school band concert with every piece starting in F Major! Surprisingly, it never came to my attention until just a few weeks prior to the performance. At that point, it was too late to adjust the program. From an educational standpoint, this eliminated the opportunity for my students to learn and perform in multiple keys. In addition, from the standpoint of the audience members, the evening proved to be a bit tedious (to say the least!).

⓮ Flowchart of Entire Piece

To further clarify and mentally synthesize the overall structure, your next step in the study of your score is to create a flowchart or diagram of the piece. Using a pencil and a blank piece of paper, begin to "map" the piece from measure 1 to its conclusion at measure 63. Important items that should appear in your flowchart include:

a) Rehearsal letters
b) Measure numbers (that match those you have written into your score)
c) Time signature(s)
d) Tempo markings
e) Structural sections of the piece and where they occur (These should include thematic development.)
f) Phrase sections of the themes (indicated by the use of lower case letters such as a, b, c, etc.)
g) Orchestration and texture
h) Style of various sections of the work
i) Instrument families or combinations of instruments playing
j) General dynamic markings as they unfold
k) Key centers, basic harmonic progressions, and important cadences

Appendix C is an example of a simple flowchart for *Flourish for Wind Band.* It is recommended that you use this, or a similar example, as a model from which to base your own flowcharts. Complete this important exercise for virtually every piece you ever prepare to conduct in the future.

Once again, be reminded that one of the principal reasons for score study is to vividly synthesize an aural rendering of the entire composition in your head. When a conductor has a thorough comprehension and cerebral recording of the work embedded mentally, it enables him or her to rehearse with conviction, decisiveness and effectiveness.

⓯ Marked & Prepared Score

Marking your conductor's score is a critical stage in score and rehearsal preparation. It should reflect thorough study and planning as you prepare to begin rehearsing each new work.

The three principal reasons for meticulously marking and preparing your score are as follows:

a) To help you to create an informed interpretation and vivid image of the piece in your own mind from which to aspire.

b) To make editorial corrections and necessary "retouchings" of the score and/or parts. These may include substituting instruments when deemed necessary, to edit the edition for historical authenticity, or to simplify passages when necessary to accommodate the skill level of your musicians.

c) To assist you in the running of effective, efficient rehearsals and during actual podium conducting.

This procedure is very personal and philosophies regarding this important process vary significantly among highly respected conductors and pedagogues. Some advise using very few or no markings at all, while others recommend the extensive use of colored pencils and highlighter pens. Some recommend the purchase of two full scores, one for detailed analysis and the other for podium use. As you experiment with this process, you will begin to develop a style and procedure that works best for you.

Score markings fall into three basic categories:

a) Structural, melodic, motivic and harmonic analysis of the piece (as you have already begun to address),

b) Those critical markings that represent your *own* interpretation (metronome markings, phrasing, breath marks, bowings, articulation, stick or mallet preferences, etc.), and

c) Those referring to significant events in the music that will assist you to rehearse and conduct the piece effectively (entrances, time signature changes, fermatas, caesuras, pauses, repeats, subdivided beats, groupings of asymmetrical meters, descriptive phrases or analogies to help emote your desired interpretation of a passage, and hard-to-read measure numbers or rehearsal letters).

Most conductors who find value in marking their scores for rehearsal purposes do seem to agree upon the following basic guidelines:

a) Mark you scores rather sparingly so that they remain easily readable.

b) Your principal marking tool should be a soft, dark pencil (No. 2). Pencil instead of pen will make it much easier to erase or make changes if and when necessary.

c) Use RED pencil to indicate important cues and entrances so that they stand out and are *easily* spotted as you take a quick look down at your score. Use sizeable "brackets" placing these critical markings where they can be easily "spotted," and to where your eyes naturally gravitate on the written page.

d) Next to those entrances, indicate the entering instrument(s) using a standard abbreviation. Again, make these clear, *legible* and prominent enough that your eyes will easily be able to locate and read them at a glance. (Note that some conductors prefer to print each of the letters in these abbreviations in CAPITAL or upper case letters.) See Appendix D for a listing of standard instrument abbreviations.

e) Any important information that is difficult to read due to its print size or somewhat hidden location on the score should be enlarged, in most cases using a colored pencil. These may include tempo markings, meter changes, rehearsal letters or measure numbers, clef changes, specific mute requests, repeats and codas, and critical tempo changes such as ritardandos, rallentandos, or accelerandos.

f) Highlighter pens should be used discreetly. They are most often used to effectively draw attention to dynamic changes. It is recommended that you limit your use to YELLOW markers so that the original print always remains easily readable through the highlighted shading.

g) When more than one staff is printed on a single page, it is always wise to separate those staves by either using a wavy line between them or by printing a large, prominent // at the beginning and end of the lines of music. Utilizing one of these suggestions will help prevent your eyes from skipping a complete line of music while conducting.

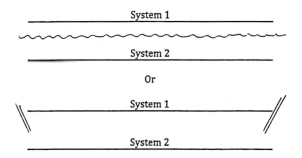

Additional recommended sources that include specific suggestions for use when marking your score include *Lead and Inspire* by Robert J. Garofalo and Frank L. Battisti, and *On Becoming a Conductor* by Frank L. Battisti. As you begin establishing your own score marking habits and style, it would be wise to refer to these important texts and adopt those suggestions that work best for you.

Congratulations! You have completed Phase Two!

PHASE III

INTERPRETATION AND PREPARATION FOR THE INITIAL REHEARSAL

⓰ Sang Through, Studied & Marked Each Individual Part in Score for Phrasing and Breath Marks

From the piccolo to the string bass part, every conductor should be able to sing each part with the phrasing and breath marks that he or she has determined are appropriate. In addition, percussion parts should also be "sung" as to phrasing, nuances, stick or mallet choices and possible adjusted dynamic markings.

To hone your sight singing skills, use the piano as little as possible while going through each part. Remember that, in addition to learning to sing the "right notes and rhythms," you should be equally concerned with the rise, fall and direction of each melodic line, the "space" (or lack thereof) between the notes, the appropriate musical emphasis on certain pitches or rhythmic figures, and the best places to ask the musicians to breathe that don't interfere with the continuity of each line of the music. These are critical decisions that must be made prior to the first rehearsal. Otherwise, you run the risk of wasting valuable rehearsal time as you either seek to make those decisions "on the spot," or fail to address these musical issues altogether!

Whenever addressing a new concept, remember that you have the choice of insisting that the notes and/or rhythms be played correctly from the start or find yourself "correcting" the errors later on that have by then been "learned" incorrectly. Veteran teachers know that it is significantly easier to "teach" than to "correct!" However, in order to do this, it is absolutely necessary that you have made each of those decisions in advance of the day the new piece is introduced in rehearsal.

Breath marks should be indicated at musically appropriate spots in the music utilizing a mark similar to an apostrophe (') or, as some prefer, a "check mark" (✓). When rests are provided appropriately in the music, breath marks are not necessary. In addition, the rise and fall of each melodic line can be indicated in your score with the use of arrows going up or down, or "dotted line" crescendos or diminuendos. The latter are often referred to as "intensity crescendos" or "intensity diminuendos" with the understanding that they are to be subtle nuances and not sweeping dynamic changes. As you meticulously complete this step with each instrumental part, place a check mark on its corresponding line of the *Score & Rehearsal Preparation Worksheet*. Again, *you are not ready to begin rehearsing the piece until after you have completed this crucially important step with each and every instrument, including the percussion parts.*

⑰ Seating Recommendations

Determining the best possible seating arrangement for your concert band, wind ensemble, orchestra or chamber ensemble can make a significant impact on the overall blend, balance, pitch and precision of your group. A list of factors to consider when formulating the best possible ensemble seating should include size and acoustical characteristics of your rehearsal hall and concert stage, strengths and weaknesses of individual players and sections, the number of players on each part, the demands of each piece being programmed, and your personal overall desired tonal concept.

Concert Band and Wind Ensemble Seating
The following are the generally agreed upon "fundamental principles" of wind band seating as articulated by Russell Pizer (*How to Improve the High School Band Sound*, Parker Publishing Company, 1976). Also included is a carefully gleaned list of specific suggestions offered by some of the recognized legends of our profession.

Fundamental Principles of Wind Band Seating

1. Seat all players in such a way that they can see the conductor — a must!
2. Seat like instruments together.
3. Seat large sections in a block (or row).
4. Seat instruments playing the same (or similar) parts in close proximity to each other.
5. Seat players playing principal parts in close proximity. (A very large concert band may be the possible exception to this rule.) Place instruments so that their tone is projected in its most advantageous manner.

6. Place instruments neither where their projection overburdens the total balance of the group nor in such a place that they must force their tone to be heard.

Specific Suggestions to Consider

1. **Avoid placing too many flutes in the first row!** More than about six flutes placed in the first row will probably result in a "top heavy" overall band sound and make the desired balance virtually impossible. When faced with the common public school dilemma of having too many flutes, you may wish to consider splitting the section into multiple partial rows, placing those extra flutists on one side of the band.

    Depending on the relative size and strength of your wind ensemble flute and clarinet sections, you may find it advantageous to place your clarinets in the front row and the flutes in the second. Robert Garofalo (*Improving Intonation in Band and Orchestra Performance,* Meredith Music Publications, 1996) advocates placing the clarinets in the first row on a regular basis. This pronounces the clarinets as the prominent nucleus of tone in the ensemble, similar to the violin section in a symphony orchestra.

    It's also interesting to note that in his 1988 recording of marches with the Tokyo Kosei Wind Orchestra, Frederick Fennell also placed his entire clarinet section in the front row.

2. **Be sure to place the French horns in the optimal location.** The horns must always be seated in a spot where they a) can be readily heard by the trumpet section for the sake of tuning and sound mix, b) can be easily heard throughout the auditorium, and c) have their bells generally directed *away* from any audience members so that their preferred "veiled" sound quality is preserved.

    Howard Hilliard ("Alternative Horn Placement," *The Instrumentalist,* October, 2004) suggests that placing the horns squarely in the middle of your ensemble may *not* always prove to be the best spot for purposes of projection. To maintain the characteristic "veiled" horn sound while still reaping the benefits of strong projection, experiment with placing the horns *slightly* to the right or left side of your band. Remember that if placed on the left, the horn bells must not point directly towards any audience members. The acoustics of your hall will need to be considered as you make a final decision in this regard.

    For the purpose of tuning and matching tone quality it is also imperative that *the principal horn player's bell be pointed in the general direction of the rest of the section in both bands and orchestras.* If they are arranged in a row, the principal horn player should be seated to the left of the rest of the section or on the conductor's right (IV III II I).

3. **Be sure to seat the horns and saxophones near each other.** Due to the frequent similarity of their parts and their frequent need to resolve differences in pitch, the saxophones and horns should be seated in very close proximity to each other. A common general preference is for the principal alto saxophone to be seated next to or very nearby the principal horn.

Horns   *Saxophones*

IV   III   II   I   1st Alto   2nd Alto   Tenor   Baritone

4. **Seat the bassoons, bass clarinets, and euphoniums so that they can be heard from the audience.** Consider placing the bassoons, bass clarinets and/or euphoniums on the outside of their respective rows or near the edge of the stage to enhance their audibility. This may not be possible for all three sections so consider the relative strengths and weaknesses of each section and the prominence of their individual parts in each selection on the concert program. *Don't be afraid to move them around from piece to piece.*

5. **The trumpet sound must not overpower the rest of the band.** The alarming truth about this frequent problem is that the band director, from his or her vantage point, is often totally unaware that there is a problem. To avoid an overpowering and unblended trumpet sound, consider placing the trumpets and cornets near the rear and slightly off to the side of the ensemble. The backs of the other instrumentalists seated in front of them will serve to filter their sound and the off-center placement will enhance their overall blend within the band.

     W. Francis McBeth ("Please Be Seated," *The Instrumentalist*, September, 2000) explains that if the trumpets are placed on the outside, extreme left of your ensemble, the overall blend may sound OK to the conductor, but the front right side of the audience may be hearing straight trumpet sound!

6. **Seat bass instruments in reasonable proximity to each other in order to achieve a solid, unified sound.** Garofalo also suggests placing the tubas, euphoniums, contra and bass clarinets, baritone saxophone, string bass, timpani and bass drum on the right side of the standard wind ensemble.

     Harry Begian ("Experiments in Band Seating," *The Instrumentalist*, December, 1997) suggests placing these same bass instruments down the middle of the ensemble. In either scenario, the bass instruments are placed so that they can hear one another. This is critical if your band is to achieve the desired pyramid of sound, as eloquently advocated by W. Francis McBeth (*Effective Performance of Band Music*, Southern Music, 1972).

7. **Place the tubas, timpani and bass drum close together.** Lynn G. Cooper (*Teaching Band & Orchestra: Methods and Materials*, GIA Publication, 2004) recommends placing the tubas and timpani next to each other in order to improve the fundamental pitch accuracy of the ensemble, and also placing the bass drum near the timpani for enhanced rhythmic cohesion. Separating the bass drum and timpani may result in a lack of rhythmic definition, especially when performing most 20th and 21st century repertoire.

8. **Place the keyboard percussion instruments where they can be easily heard.** In his 1972 text, W. Francis McBeth suggests placing the mallet percussion instruments (chimes, xylophone, marimba, and vibraphone) near the edge of the stage or on the outside of the percussion section for best sound projection.

9. **Don't be reluctant to alter your seating plan from piece to piece.** Vary the seating of your wind ensemble or concert band whenever a rearrangement will enhance the overall balance, blend, projection or precision of a specific piece.

   Robert Curry ("Changing Seating To Suit the Music," *The Instrumentalist*, December 1994) states, "The music should dictate the seating." Jeffrey Renshaw ("Seating Bands for the Music," *The Instrumentalist*, October, 2000) adds, "With the diversity of modern band repertoire, conductors should use different seating arrangements for different styles of music...."

   The two sections of the band most frequently and positively affected by such seating changes are the cornets/trumpets (due to the varying number of parts from piece to piece) and the percussion. Programming a piece requiring only three cornet parts immediately followed by a work with three cornet and two trumpet parts may necessitate a change in seating in that section.

   In regard to your percussion section, the specific demands of the individual parts may dictate exactly how the instruments should be arranged. For example, consider placing the snare drum and timpani side-by-side when performing Claude T. Smith's *God of Our Fathers* for significantly enhanced precision in the Allegretto and the fugue sections. To instantly improve the rhythmic precision and balance in the pesky vibes and bells parts in Gillingham's *Be Thou My Vision*, place those two keyboard percussion instruments and their players next to each other.

10. **Avoid rehearsing exclusively on risers, and then performing on a flat stage.** If your wind ensemble or concert band rehearses on risers, be sure that they also perform on risers on the concert stage. Failure to heed this advice may result in balance and ensemble problems during your dress rehearsal and concert performance.

If your group is planning to perform at an upcoming concert, competition or festival without risers, be sure to spend sufficient time rehearsing on a flat stage prior to your performance or competition. Heeding this advice alone will safeguard the director from countless "surprises" and "headaches."

11. **Don't be reluctant to alter your basic seating plan from year to year.** If your instrumentation (or perhaps just the strengths and weaknesses within each section) tends to vary each semester or concert season, adjust your seating arrangement to compensate for those changes. Very few directors have the luxury of conducting an ensemble that is always 100% consistent in the above criteria and your basic seating blueprint should reflect those fluctuations.

12. **Be sure to get off the podium and listen to your group from the auditorium seats.** It is imperative that the conductor spend sufficient time listening to the band or wind ensemble from **various** locations around the auditorium.

    McBeth further writes in his article in *The Instrumentalist*, "When experimenting with seating, try getting back a distance from the band and listen." It is indeed astounding just how different your group may sound from the audience!

    Follow all the guidelines above and then be sure to devote a significant portion of at least one rehearsal experimenting with your seating plan for each piece and listening to your group from different vantage points all over the auditorium. This practice will prove to be worth every minute of "lost" rehearsal time and should result in much more successful concert performances.

    Appendix E includes the "standard" seating plans utilized by a number of highly respected wind band conductors from public school to professional service band. In addition, you will find an excellent collection of wind band seating charts in *On Becoming a Conductor* by Frank L. Battisti.

    In regard to *Flourish for Wind Band*, a standard seating plan should suffice. However, be sure to consider each and every factor addressed above. A possible seating plan variation to consider is the possibility of arranging the players in somewhat of an antiphonal seating, as suggested in the article by author Stuart Stone ("The Flowing Lines of Flourish for Wind Band," *The Instrumentalist*, June 1999). Placing the horns and trombones opposite the cornets and trumpets (either on opposing sides of the stage or in two different locations in the auditorium) should achieve this unique effect. Such spatial arrangements sometimes create ensemble problems due to time lag, so be sure to allow time to rehearse and adjust this creative seating well in advance of the concert performance.

Symphony Orchestra Seating

The seating for orchestras is somewhat more standard depending upon the time period during which each piece to be performed was composed. However, avid concertgoers will discover some variation in the seating arrangements, even among professional symphony orchestras.

Fundamental Principles of Symphony Orchestra Seating

1. **Seat the strings in front of the winds and percussion.** Though it's common to find the flutes, oboes and/or clarinets in the front row in a wind band, it's extremely unusual to find any instruments but the strings in the front portion of an orchestra.
2. **Seat the violins, violi and celli in "columns" or "files" proceeding back from the podium AND in** pairs **(two to a music stand).** Unlike bands and wind ensembles, these three string instrument families are almost never seated in rows from left to right of like instruments.
3. **Place the first violins to the left of the conductor with the concertmaster on the front corner nearest the edge of the stage.** There are precious few "absolutes" in this world, but this may be one of them!
4. **Either place the second violins slightly to the right and directly adjacent to the first violins with the principal chair in the front of the column directly in front of the conductor (on the left side of the front pair) OR place the entire section to the right of the conductor nearest the edge of the stage.** Here lies one of the few standard variations sometimes found in orchestral seating. You will notice both practices represented in the accompanying seating charts. When adopting the latter seating, be sure to place the principal 2nd violinist on the outside nearest the edge of the stage. (Note that the latter practice was common during the Mozart/Haydn era.)
5. **More commonly found is the placing of the cello section to the right of the conductor with the principal player nearest the edge of the stage.** Again, this is not an absolute, but seems to be the most prevalent seating of this important section of the string family. Once again, be sure to seat the celli in columns and pairs proceeding back from the conductor.
6. **Place the violi in columns and pairs to the left and adjacent to the celli.** Again, please note the slight variation in the seating most often used when placing this "alto" member of the string section.
7. **String basses are almost always placed to the right side of the stage in a row (or occasionally two rows) directly behind the celli or 2nd violins.** Once again, the principal player is placed at the end of this row nearest the edge of the stage.

8. **Woodwinds are generally placed in two small rows straight back from the conductor within the "V-shaped wedge" between the inside string sections. The 2–3 flutes/piccolo and 2–3 oboes/ English horn are placed in the front row and the 2–3 clarinets/ bass clarinet and 2–3 bassoons/contrabassoon in the second row directly behind. The principal players in each of these sections are generally placed on the inside directly adjacent to each other.**

9. **Brass are commonly placed on either side of the woodwinds or behind them.** Acoustics of the hall can have a heavy influence in the determination of their placement, as can the particular preference of the conductor.

10. **Place the horns in the optimal location so that they can be heard sufficiently.** Be sure to read the recommendations in the band seating section regarding horn placement. The very same guidelines apply to an orchestral seating plan. In addition, an Assistant Principal Horn is usually placed to the right of the principal horn or on the opposite side from the second horn.

11. **Percussion are either placed in the back or on either side of the orchestra.** Once again, auditorium acoustics play a significant role in determining the best possible placement of the percussion section. Always avoid placing them in any spot on the stage where they can sound overbearing.

Again, please refer to Appendix E for some standard seating charts of reputable symphony orchestras. These should prove as models as you seek to determine the most advantageous seating for each piece you plan to program.

⓲ Percussion Parts Determined and Assigned

The distribution of percussion parts is more complicated than for any other section in the ensemble, especially in much of the standard wind band literature. A tremendous amount of time (and confusion) can be saved during early rehearsals if these parts are carefully scrutinized and assigned to specific players in advance. For public school, community and some collegiate ensembles, it is recommended that the conductor personally make these part assignments. For more advanced and/or professional groups, this important task can be delegated to a responsible percussion section leader or principal percussionist. There are a series of reasons why the conductor of non-professional ensembles should be responsible for this important task prior to the first rehearsal.

a) By going through this process, the conductor will become keenly aware of the particular percussion instruments required, as well as the exact number of percussion players needed to perform each piece. If dealing with a large section, he or she may also choose to split up a few parts to afford more student percussionists the opportunity to play.

b) Though the timpani music is usually printed separately, it is very common for more than one percussion part (snare drum, bass drum, cymbals, etc.) to be printed on the same sheet of music. It is not always obvious "who should play what." If the music is simply distributed at the beginning of the first rehearsal, you may find the percussionists struggling to play all the instruments as they attempt to determine how to best cover each part.

c) With developing players, a wise conductor will want to make sure that each of the members of this important section are being provided the opportunity to become "complete" or "total" percussionists. This necessitates that each player be provided performance experience on all of the primary percussion instruments. These include timpani, keyboard percussion, snare drum, bass drum, cymbals, and the accessory instruments. If the assignment of parts is left to the young students themselves, there is no guarantee that this objective will be addressed.

d) Assigning all percussion parts for the upcoming concert also assures that each student is being afforded an equitable number of parts and pieces. Make sure that no percussionist is treated unfairly.

e) If the conductor makes the assignments, he or she can also make sure that the most proficient players are placed on the most challenging parts. This may prove important as the ensemble prepares for especially critical concerts, festivals or competitions.

To accomplish this task, the conductor should sit down with the full score and a copy of each individual percussion part. Make a list of each of the instruments required and begin to discern the assignment of each part. Looking at the Vaughan Williams *Flourish...*, you will notice that there are just two separate parts (Timpani and Percussion). The timpani part is written separate from any other parts. However, the Percussion part seems to include snare drum, cymbal and bass drum.

Look down through the Percussion part to see if there are any times when all three instruments are asked to play simultaneously. You will notice that this is, indeed, the case at A, 1 before B, C, the 5th of C and elsewhere. If your ensemble has at least four percussionists, the assignments for this piece will be simple. Assign one player to each of the four parts.

Next, make a chart of your percussion part assignments. In its simplest form, it can look like this:

Vaughan Williams
    Timpani   —   **Geoff**
    Snare Drum —   **Kara**
    Cymbal   —   **Kirstie**
    Bass Drum   —   **Matt**

Two more formal looking percussion assignment charts can be found in Appendix F.

Add the assignments for all of the other pieces to be performed on the upcoming concert(s) on this same "chart." Post this chart in various places such as on the percussion cabinet, on a rehearsal bulletin board, etc. It would also be wise to write each of the appropriate musician names on their respective parts in pencil prior to distribution. This will serve as further confirmation as to whom each part has been assigned.

In regard to the Vaughan Williams work, one other determination needs to be made. The publisher lists "cymbal" as one of the instruments. Does this mean suspended cymbal or a pair of crash cymbals? One "clue" might be the lack of any rolls in the part. Another might be the musical nature of a fanfare or "flourish" which often uses cymbal crashes at key cadence points. With these two criteria in mind, it appears that Vaughan Williams probably intended this part to be performed with a pair of crash cymbals. An additional suggestion to consider is the possible use of both as occasionally recommended by Anthony Cirone in his outstanding text (*On Musical Interpretation in Percussion Performance: A Study of Notation and Musicianship*, Meredith Music Publication, 2008).

Such lack of clarity is not uncommon in percussion part writing. Other such ambiguities include the call for "gong" (which is a pitched instrument) rather than the intended non-pitched "tam-tam." Another is the part assigned to the "glockenspiel" (a rather antiquated lyre shaped marching band instrument) rather than the intended "orchestra bells."

It should be noted that the part assignments for *Flourish for Wind Band* were very quick and easy in comparison to many other standard works you will encounter. Plan to devote some time to this important task for each piece you program with your ensemble. Doing this in advance of your first rehearsal will pay "big dividends" in regard to rehearsal efficiency, as well as make significant strides in the development of the "complete percussionists" under your tutelage.

An enormously helpful resource for the non-percussionist wind band conductor is the two-volume set by Russ Girsberger entitled *Percussion Assignments for Band & Wind Ensemble* which will help you to make percussion part assignments for most of the standard concert band repertoire for middle to college bands. Equally valuable is his *A Practical Guide to Percussion Terminology*. Both can be found in the Selective Bibliography at the back of this text.

⑲ Solo/Soli/Section Parts Assigned

Another important task that must be addressed prior to the first reading of a piece is to make a list of each and every solo, soli or reduced instrumentation passage and assign those parts to specific players in your ensemble. Making these assignments either verbally or with a posting on your bulletin board alleviates confusion among the musicians and guarantees that the individuals of your choice are performing each of those passages. If done at least a few days prior to the first rehearsal, it also provides those designated soloists the opportunity to practice those passages in advance.

Though it may seem that principal players should "automatically" play every solo, you may determine that certain solos are a better fit for someone else in the section. For instance, if you are programming either the orchestral or wind band edition of Bernstein's *Slava!,* you may determine that your second or third chair trumpet and/or trombone player is much more comfortable performing in the vaudeville solo style required by the composer. This would be an excellent opportunity to afford these individuals the chance to "shine" on that particular series of solos.

Some conductors in educational settings also are in the practice of routinely giving solos to a variety of young musicians. Again, in order to have the opportunity to make these decisions in a fair and contemplative manner, this task must be addressed during the initial score and rehearsal preparation process.

㉒ Errors Corrected in Score & Parts

Taking the time to correct the known errors in the score and in each individual part before distribution will save an immeasurable amount of frustration and rehearsal time. Lists of errata can often be found in professional journal articles devoted to the preparation of the specific piece. These include *The Instrumentalist,* the long-since discontinued *BD Guide*, in a number of the chapters found in the *Conductors Anthology*, and at the conclusion of some of the chapters devoted to many of the large instrumental works found in the GIA series *Teaching Musicianship Through Performance in Orchestra* (and *Band*). In addition, such lists exist on various internet sites.

For conductors of concert bands and wind ensembles, another valuable resource is the series entitled *Errata Studies for the Wind Band Conductor* by Timothy Topolewsky. In this five-volume set, Dr. Topolewsky addresses many of the standard wind band works containing an especially long (and embarrassing) list of publisher errors in the score and parts.

This critical but tedious job can be delegated to section leaders, librarians, or graduate assistants. However, if you skip this step entirely in your preparation for the initial reading of a piece, you may find yourself entertaining a plethora of "raised hands" and accompanying grimaces on the faces of your musicians, and may be forced to discern the corrections while the rehearsal "clock is ticking."

Please note that in more up-to-date editions of significant works, many of the initial errors may have been corrected. As long as the new edition is true to the composer, these editions should be sought. Examples include the Frederick Fennell edition of *Lincolnshire Posy* for wind band by Percy Grainger, as well as the Colin Matthews edition of the Gustav Holst *First Suite in Eb for Military Band.*

In regard to *Flourish for Wind Band*, it appears that few if any errors have been found in its brief 63 measures. None of the articles we have examined include any list of errata whatsoever. However, it will be wise to keep a blank piece of paper readily available during rehearsals to record any errors that may become apparent. Keeping such a list will prove valuable for performances of the piece in later years, as well as when asked to serve as a guest conductor with festival ensembles on such pieces.

㉑ Anticipated Trouble Spots & Planned Rehearsal Strategies/ Lesson Plan

Every conscientious conductor and educator will spend a lifetime seeking new and more effective rehearsal strategies to add to his or her "arsenal." This is a never-ending quest and there are no "shortcuts" to this lifelong endeavor. Some basic rehearsal techniques may be employed on a rather routine basis, but many others will need to be specific and relevant to the particular work and/or passage that is being addressed.

The Selective Bibliography found in the back of this text lists a number of outstanding resources. However, I will attempt to provide a "must" list for young aspiring conductors that may help to serve as a basis from which to build. Please note that this list is compiled in alphabetical order by author.

Boonshaft, Peter Loel, *Teaching Music with Passion.* This is an insightful text that continues to inspire its readers at all levels of music making.

Casey, Joseph L., *Teaching Techniques and Insights for Instrumental Music.* Organized by topic, approximately 138 successful instrumental music teachers from the elementary to collegiate level offer specific suggestions for effective teaching techniques and rehearsal strategies.

McBeth, W. Francis, *Effective Performance of Band Music* Dr. McBeth's chapter on the Double Pyramid Balance System is legendary.

Garofalo, Robert J., *Improving Intonation in Band and Orchestra Performance.* This is one of the definitive texts on the topic.

Labuta, Joseph A., *Basic Conducting Techniques.* Chapter 13, "The Instrumental Rehearsal," addresses the basics of rehearsal techniques and planning. It serves as an excellent introduction to this important topic.

Lisk, Edward S., *The Creative Director: Conductor, Teacher, Leader.* This is also an outstanding source and should be recommended reading in every instrumental methods class. His other texts are also recommended.

Williamson, John E., *Rehearsing the Band.* This informative text is comprised of chapters by eleven legendary university wind band conductors. Much can be gleaned from the informative pages of this significant paperback.

Look through the pages of the Vaughan Williams score and begin to make a list of probable problematic passages, saving the addition of possible rehearsal strategies until later. Note, of course, that your list of designated trouble spots will be longer if you are conducting a younger and less accomplished group of musicians. Remember, too, that some specific passages may have been identified in the articles or chapters you have already studied about the preparation of the piece. Be sure to heed those "warnings" and suggestions during this important phase of your initial rehearsal preparation.

Vaughan Williams Flourish for Wind Band

Probable Problematic Passages

1. If you are using an early edition of this piece, it may be necessary to teach your 1st and 2nd trombones to read tenor clef.
2. Young brass students may need to be admonished to count carefully in the imitation sections at the opening of the work, and again beginning at measure 45. The fact that some of their entrances are different in the repeat of the A section may result in some inaccurate entrances.
3. Balance in the trumpets and cornets may become problematic when the parts divide at measures 8–10, 22–23, 26–27, 30–31, 33–35, 42–45, 51–53, and 61–63.
4. The key changes at 19 and 40 may result in some wrong notes.
5. A common error is for musicians to inadvertently slow the tempo during soft passages. Prepare for this possibility as you approach letter B.
6. The rather isolated scoring of moving eighth notes within the tutti sections at 25, 27, 31, 33 will probably get "swallowed up" if not brought out.
7. The critical, but lightly scored moving quarters in the alto saxophones and euphoniums at 39 will probably need to be brought out.
8. The frequent overlapping of phrases throughout will probably need to be drilled to prevent premature releases.

With younger ensembles, balance, rhythmic clarity, note length, phrasing nuances, intonation, lack of attention to printed dynamics and maintaining a supported sound during soft passages are all possible problems to further anticipate.

Your next step is to carefully plan the specific rehearsal and/or teaching strategies you will employ to address each of the probable problems above. Every successful athletic coach adopts a "game plan" prior to every game and conductors must do the same.

Planned Rehearsal/Teaching Strategies

1. To address the tenor clef with the trombones, it would be wise to introduce it in group or private lessons or in sectionals weeks before the first

reading of the piece. (You could also rewrite their parts to avoid the use of the tenor clef, but this would also deny them the opportunity to learn this important clef.)

2. The strategy of "repetition" is often one of the conductor's "best friends" when it comes to beneficial teaching techniques. In the brass fanfare sections, be sure to verbally point out the differences in the two A section passages and then practice them both multiple times to engrain their slight dissimilarities into the minds of the performing musicians.

3. Since lower frequencies and/or passages often sound softer (as is the case with some of these particular trumpet passages), encourage those playing the lower parts to bolster their dynamic level a bit to audibly match the upper lines. It should also be noted that balance problems within an instrument section can sometimes be helped by "stacking" the assignment of parts if you have a sufficient numbers of players. (This means placing more players on the lower parts so that they sound balanced with the upper parts.) However, in the case of these trumpet passages, this is probably not feasible or advisable.

4. If dealing with young players, design and lead your ensemble through some creative warm-up scale drills at the beginning of the rehearsal that teach and reinforce the keys of F and Bb concert. Then be sure to point out that these are the exact keys for which they will be asked to perform at those critical transitions in the music.

5. Sensitize the musicians to the fact that slow passages often have the tendency to slow down. One popular strategy is to amplify a steady metronome at the front of the rehearsal hall throughout the soft passages to help the students to maintain a steady tempo. Another creative technique is to have the students audibly sing their parts going in and out of the B section while the conductor holds a beating metronome in his hand. At various and unannounced moments, turn the metronome to "mute" as the musicians continue to sing. Every few measures or so, turn the metronome volume back on to see if the student musicians have been successful at maintaining the tempo. With subsequent repetitions of this drill, wait longer and longer in mute mode before turning the volume back on. This can prove to be a very effective strategy for placing the responsibility of steady tempo upon the shoulders of the musicians in your ensemble (and not on the conductor or the bass drummer!).

6. Begin by asking the students with the moving notes in question to circle those passages in their parts. You may also have to ask everyone else to hold back a bit and to listen for those moving lines. Tell the others that if they can't hear those critical notes, then they are probably playing too loudly. Rehearse those spots until the moving lines are projected sufficiently. In addition, in your private conducting practice sessions in

front of a mirror, pretend to be "cuing" each of those instruments and always look in their direction at those critical moments.

7. Approach the moving quarter note passages in exactly the same manner as you did with the eighths above.

8. During the preparation of step 16 on your *Score & Rehearsal Preparation Worksheet,* be sure to address breath marks in every section and the length of final notes of all phrases. Write these markings into their individual parts, or dictate them to your musicians early in the rehearsing of the piece. Drill and "repetition" of the most critical passages in regard to phrase overlaps should prove effective in creating the flow of the lines as intended by the composer. Once again, during your solitary conducting practice sessions, remember to address your determined phrase releases in your conducting along with accompanying glances in the direction of the instrument families most affected. One final suggestion is to keep a list of your most successful rehearsal strategies either printed in your personal score or on a separate piece of paper attached to your *Score & Rehearsal Preparation Worksheet.* These will prove enormously valuable whenever you get this or any other piece out again in subsequent years for another performance. Again, "why reinvent the wheel?!"

㉒ Memorized Rehearsal Spots (list here)

One of the benefits of preparing your scores utilizing this systematic approach is that you will find it increasingly less necessary to keep your eyes "buried" in the music. This freedom from being "chained" to the score affords the conductor the opportunity to maintain better eye contact, as well as the ability to be less distracted and better hear the intricacies of the ensemble performance transpiring in front of him. However, as the conductor finds himself looking down less often during rehearsal comes the disadvantage of suddenly losing his place in the music. In a continued effort to use your precious rehearsal time most efficiently and to keep the pace of your rehearsal "moving," consider memorizing a few key rehearsal spots. With a few key spots memorized by rehearsal letter or measure number, you can quickly ask the musicians to start at a specific spot without having to flip pages thus slowing the valuable momentum you have created.

This can be done in one of two ways. First, you can memorize a few key spots by rehearsal letter. In the Vaughan Williams, memorize spots as follows:

Memorized Rehearsal Spots by Rehearsal Letter

A = tutti section where the woodwinds and remaining brass and percussion join the horns, cornets, trumpets and trombones.
B = the beginning of the soft section in the key of F Major

5th of C = the key change back to Bb
D = return of the tutti section similar to rehearsal letter A

Another more educational (and much more interesting) way to memorize important rehearsal spots in the music is according to its *compositional form.* This can prove beneficial in three ways: 1) A few months after performing the piece, most conductors will have forgotten rehearsal letters and/or measure numbers. These will have to be memorized again when preparing the piece in later years. 2) The conductor is much more likely to remember key spots in a piece if linked with significant sections of the structure of the work. 3) If the musicians are informed of these important spots in the music according to the compositional form, young musicians in particular will also be afforded the opportunity to learn more about the music from the composer's viewpoint. Though it is usually difficult to determine major formal structure by only viewing their own instrument part (3rd clarinet, 3rd trumpet, snare drum, etc.), these can be dictated, learned and marked in the music by the students when incorporated in the rehearsal plan by a creative director.

During an early rehearsal, instruct the young musicians to listen and begin to identify the major sections of the work. Some instruction regarding standard compositional forms will need to be incorporated in your rehearsal plans, but this can result in increased musicianship among the students. Thus, your memorized rehearsal spots might be as follows:

Memorized Rehearsal Spots by Compositional Structure

The tutti b phrase of the intial A section = measure 11
The B section = letter B
Return of the A section = measure 45
The tutti b phrase of the return of the A Section = measure 54

In larger works, the creative conductor may identify the *exposition, development, recapitulation,* and *coda* sections of a movement in sonata allegro form. He or she might also utilize the *introduction, first strain, second strain, trio, "dog fight,"* and *trio recapitulation* of a standard march form. Though this approach will not work for every piece due to length or less obvious compositional structure, it can occasionally prove very beneficial towards maintaining a rapid rehearsal pace and, even more importantly, the musical education of the musicians themselves.

㉓ Practiced Conducting in Front of a Mirror (check off when secure)

Regular practice in a quiet, solitary room in front of a large mirror is an important step in the preparation for the first, as well as subsequent rehearsals. To be most effective, the conductor should sing the most prominent parts while conducting, give all intended cues, use facial expression and conduct all nuances precisely as he or she plans to conduct the piece in rehearsal and in the concert. It will be critically important not to conduct to a recording, but to recreate the work vocally and in your mind. This is also an excellent opportunity to practice looking down at the score only when necessary.

Like an actor, it is also wise to verbally practice how you will explain some of the interpretive nuances, as well as your planned rehearsal strategies for addressing all anticipated problems. Actors certainly rehearse their lines by talking out loud in a quiet room and this is excellent advice for teachers and conductors as well. This final stage of rehearsal planning is critical as you now are in a position to synthesize all the information you have gleaned and your systematic and comprehensive study. Rehearsing yourself carefully should result in fulfilling rehearsals for you and the fortunate musicians under your baton, and should culminate in a performance that is true to the composer's intent and musically gratifying for all in attendance.

Finale

Without excellent preparation of the score, there is no conducting.
                                                    Elizabeth A. H. Green

The conductor must have a thorough knowledge of the score and a compelling conception of how the music should sound, and be able to communicate that conception clearly and efficiently in rehearsal.
                                                    Thomas Lloyd

The sound you have in your mind is the sound you will make.
                                                    John Paynter

Only when a work has come to absolute perfection within him can he undertake to materialize it by means of the orchestra.
                                                    Hermann Scherchen

Learning the score is the ultimate mental challenge, the academic part of being a conductor.
                                                    Anthony Maiello

Without score knowledge and an image, there is no possibility of the person being an effective musical leader from the podium, regardless of the individual's proficiency at the craft of conducting.
                                                    Frank L. Battisti and Robert Garofalo

To that desired end, I challenge and encourage every conductor, no matter what the level of musicians entrusted to you, to henceforth resolve to set time aside in your daily schedule to systematically address each of the components found on the *Score and Rehearsal Preparation Worksheet* with virtually every piece you intend to conduct. After having attended to the many necessary details, remember to keep those completed worksheets along with your carefully prepared scores for all future repeat performances.

Being thoroughly prepared as you "take the podium" for every rehearsal and concert performance will significantly assist you in achieving the desired goal of aesthetic music making that will profoundly impact the souls of both the performers and your audience members alike.

May you be richly blessed as you continue on this noble quest.

S.D.G.

APPENDIX A

Symphony Orchestra Instrumentation

Violins 1 & 2
Violas
Celli
String Basses
Piccolo
Flutes 1 & 2
Oboes 1 & 2
Bassoons 1 & 2
Clarinets 1 & 2
Bass Clarinet
Trumpets 1, 2 & 3
Horns in F 1, 2, 3, 4
Trombones 1 & 2
Bass Trombone
Tuba
Timpani
Snare Drum
Bass Drum
Cymbals
Triangle
Tambourine
Orchestra Bells, Xylophone

Extra Instrumentation to be noted

Additional Piccolo Parts
Only One Flute, Oboe, Bassoon part
Flute 3
English Horn
Contrabassoon
ContraBass Clarinet
Alto Saxophone
Trumpets 1 & 2 Only or perhaps an added 4th
Horns 1 & 2 Only
Euphonium
Tuba
Piano

Harp
Celeste
Organ
Any Other Percussion Instruments

Standard Concert Band/Symphonic Wind Ensemble Instrumentation

Piccolo
Flutes 1 & 2
Oboes 1 & 2
Bassoons 1 & 2
Clarinets 1, 2, 3
Bass Clarinet
Alto Saxophones 1 & 2
Tenor Saxophone
Baritone Saxophone
Cornets 1, 2, 3
Trumpets 1 & 2
Horns in F 1, 2, 3, 4
Trombones 1 & 2
Bass Trombone
Euphoniums
Tubas
Timpani
Snare Drum
Bass Drum
Cymbals
Triangle
Tambourine
Orchestra Bells, Xylophone

Extra Instrumentation to be noted

Additional Piccolo Parts
Only One Flute, Oboe, Bassoon part
Flute 3
English Horn
Contrabassoon
Clarinet 4
ContraAlto Clarinet
ContraBass Clarinet
Soprano Saxophone
Bass Saxophone

Any Different Use of Cornets or Trumpets
Horns in Eb
Horns 1 & 2 Only
More Than 3 Trombones Needed
String Bass
Piano
Harp
Celeste
Any Other Percussion Instruments

APPENDIX B

GLOSSARY OF TERMS

Flourish for Wind Band by Ralph Vaughan Williams

a2	All (or both) parts play in unison
Ad lib.	Ad libitum. You may choose to include or omit the part
Flourish	Trumpet call or fanfare
ff	Fortissimo or Very Loud
Maestoso	Majestic, dignified
p	Piano or Soft
pp	Pianissimo or Very Soft
Ripieno	Term used in the concerto grosso of the Baroque period referring to the whole body of the orchestra, as distinct from the soloist or group of soloists (concertino).
Side Drum	British term referring to the snare drum.
Sim.	Simile. Used as a direction to continue a formula or pattern which has been indicated, such as an articulation or ornamentation.
Wind Band	Term used to indicate a full concert band that includes woodwinds, brass and percussion. Different than a British brass band.

Sources

Baker, Theodore, *Pocket-Manual of Musical Terms*. New York: G. Schirmer, 1947.

Girsberger, Russ, *A Practical Guide to Percussion Terminology*. Galesville, MD: Meredith Music Publications, 1998.

Randel, Don Michael, *Harvard Concise Dictionary of Music*. Cambridge, MA: The Belknap Press, 1978.

Westrup, J. A. and Harrison, F. Ll., *The New College Encyclopedia of Music*. New York: W. W. Norton & Company, Inc., 1960.

FLOWCHART OR MAP

Flourish for Wind Band by Ralph Vaughan Williams

	1-10	11-19	20-27	28-35	36-39	40-44	45-53	54-63
Tempo:	Maestoso							
Rehearsal Letters:		A	B		C			D
Measure Numbers:	1-10	11-19	20-27	28-35	36-39	40-44	45-53	54-63
Time Signature(s):	3/4							
Structural Sections:	A Section		B Section				A Section	
Thematic Structure:	a	b	c	d	c	c	a	b
Orchestration & Texture:	Hns. & Tbns. only Polyphonic (imitation)	Tutti Homophonic			Tutti		Hns. & Tbns. only Polyphonic (imitation)	Tutti
Style:	marcato Brass Fanfare	stately	legato / lyrical				marcato Brass Fanfare	stately
Dynamic Curve:	ff	ff > pp p/pp			< ff			
Keys, Harmony, Cadences:	Bb: V I V I	I III I VI I	F: I IV V I Half Cadence	IV I	I IV V	Bb: I IV V	V I V I	I III I VI I Authentic Cadence

59

APPENDIX D

STANDARD INSTRUMENT ABBREVIATIONS

PIC	Piccolo	COR	Cornet
FL	Flute	TPT	Trumpet
OB	Oboe	HN	Horn
EH	English Horn	TBN	Trombone
Eb CL	Eb Clarinet	BH	Baritone Horn
CL	Clarinet	EUPH	Euphonium
AC	Alto Clarinet	TUB	Tuba
BC	Bass Clarinet	VLN 1	Violin 1
CB CL	Contrabass Clarinet	VLN 2	Violin 2
BN	Bassoon	VLA	Viola
CBSN	Contrabassoon	VC	Cello
SOP	Soprano Saxophone	CB	String or ContraBass
AS	Alto Saxophone	PNO	Piano
TS	Tenor Saxophone	CEL	Celeste
BS	Baritone Saxophone	HPS	Harpsichord
		ORG	Organ
		SYNTH	Synthesizer
		HP	Harp

TIMP	Timpani
SD	Snare or Side Drum
TD	Tenor Drum
BD	Bass Drum
CC	Crash Cymbals
SC	Suspended Cymbal
TRI	Triangle
TAMB	Tambourine
WB	Wood Block
CAST	Castanets
CHIM	Chimes
XYLO	Xylophone
MAR	Marimba
VIB	Vibraphone
BELLS	Orchestra Bells or Glockenspiel
TT	Tam Tam (Unpitched Gong)
CROT	Crotales

APPENDIX E

STANDARD SYMPHONY ORCHESTRA AND CONCERT BAND/WIND ENSEMBLE SEATING ARRANGEMENTS

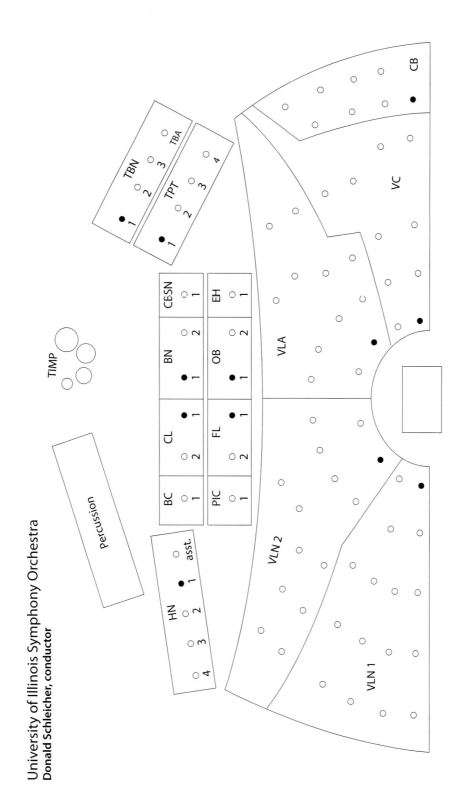

University of Illinois Symphony Orchestra
Donald Schleicher, conductor

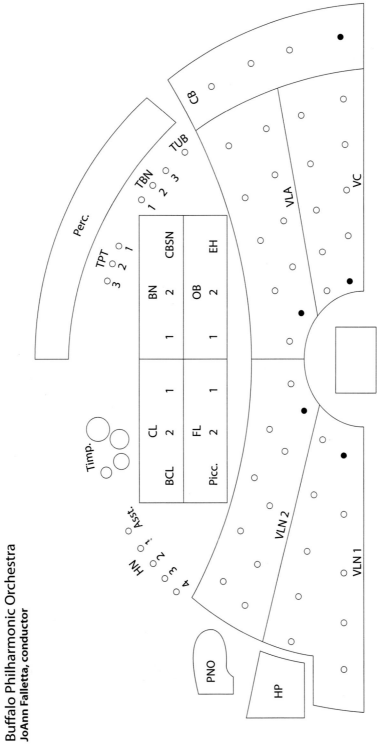

Buffalo Philharmonic Orchestra
JoAnn Falletta, conductor

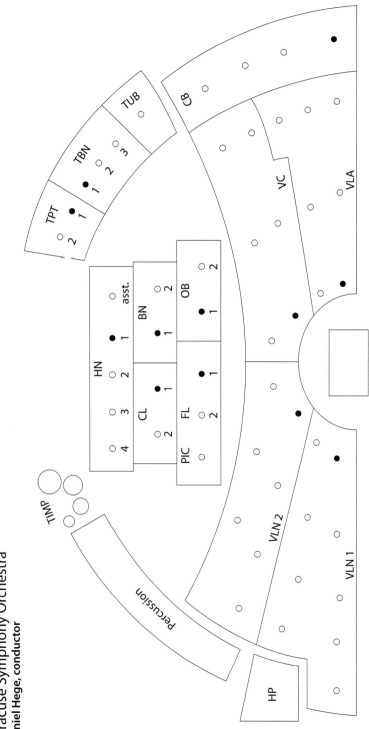

Syracuse Symphony Orchestra
Daniel Hege, conductor

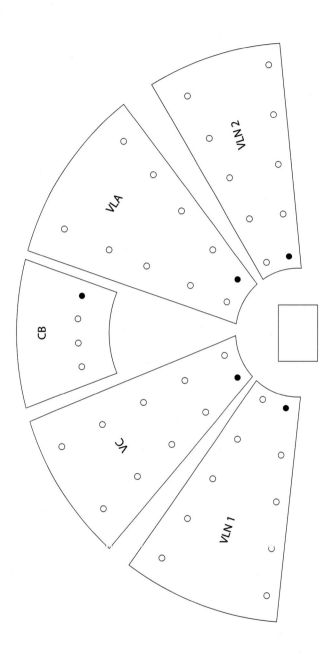

Centennial High School String Orchestra
Champaign, Illinois
Rodney Mueller, conductor

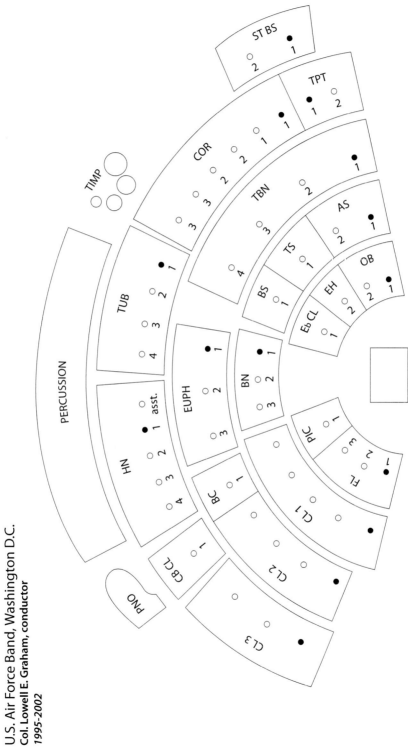

U.S. Air Force Band, Washington D.C.
Col. Lowell E. Graham, conductor
1995-2002

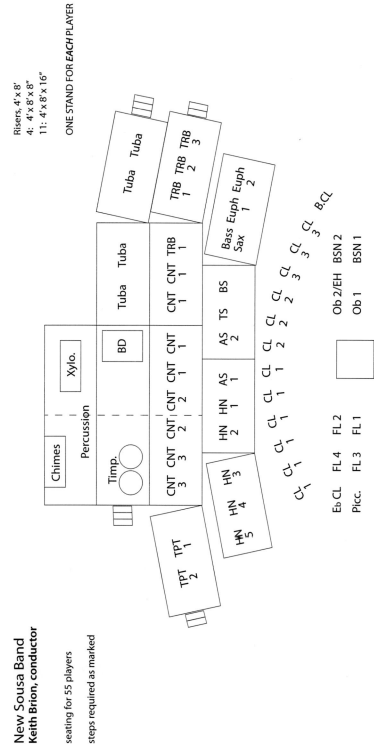

New Sousa Band
Keith Brion, conductor

seating for 55 players

steps required as marked

Risers, 4' x 8'
4: 4' x 8' x 8"
11: 4' x 8' x 16"

ONE STAND FOR *EACH* PLAYER

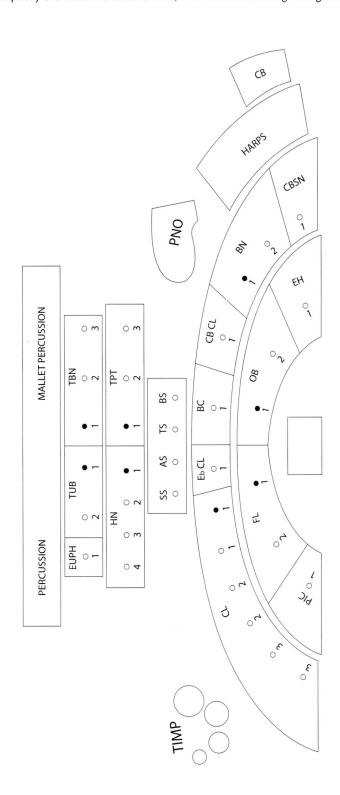

Eastman Wind Ensemble
Mark Davis Scatterday, conductor
2002 - present

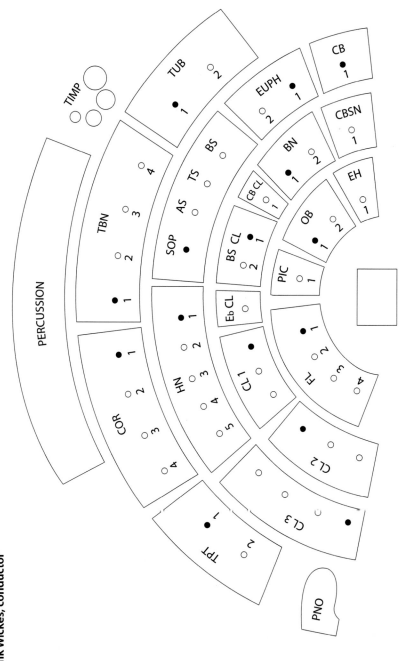

Louisiana State University Wind Ensemble
Frank Wickes, conductor

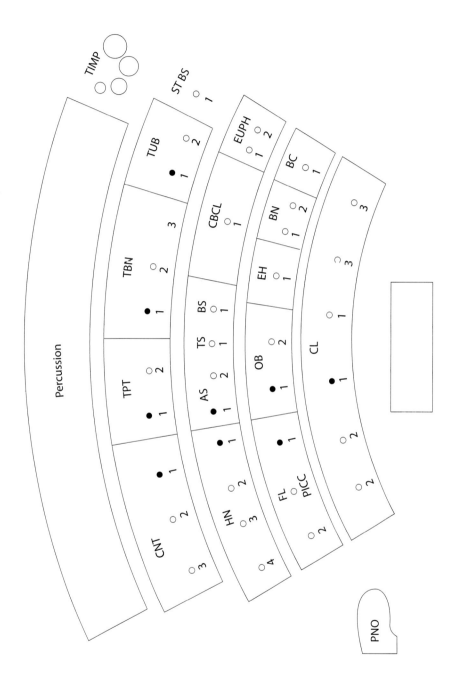

Catholic University Wind Ensemble
Robert Garofalo, conductor

Oswego High School Wind Ensemble
Edward Lisk, conductor
1973-1991

APPENDIX F

PERCUSSION ASSIGNMENT CHARTS

Houghton College Symphonic Winds
Spring Concert
Saturday, April 23, 2005

Percussion Assignments

Gillingham
Timp. — Ron
Perc. I (bells & chimes) — Sara
Perc. II (marimba & xylo.) — Geoff
Perc. III (vibes) — Matt
Perc. IV (tri, & sus. cym.) — Jill

Arnold
SD w/snares — Geoff
SD w/o snares — Matt
Cym. — Ron
BD — Sara

Stamp
Timp. — Don
Perc. I (Tam Tam, Cr. Cym. Tri.) — Ron
Perc. I (BD, Cr. Cym., Sleigh Bells, Anvil, Sus. Cym.) — Jill
Perc. II (Chimes) — Geoff
Perc. III (Vibes) — Sara
Perc. IV (Bells) — Matt

Peterson
Timp. — Ron
Perc. I (Djembe, Tam Tam, Sizzle Cym., SD, Cr. Cym., Tamborine) — Geoff
Perc. II (Crotales, Shaker, Concert Toms, BD, Tam Tam) — Jill
Perc. III (Sus., Hand Drum, Concert Toms, SD, Cr. Cym.) — Lydia
Perc. IV (Rain Stick, Wood Blocks, Shaker, Sus., Cym., Wind Chimes, Concert Toms, Whip) — Matt
Perc. V (Wind Chimes, Crotales, Finger Cym., Bells, BD) — Sara

Williamsville East High School Wind Ensemble
Percussion Assignments
Fall Concert – Thursday, November 6, 1990

Compositions Listed by Composer Names

Student Names	*Vaughan Williams*	*McBeth*	*Grainger*	*Fillmore*
Colin	Cym.	Timp.	SD	BD
Phil	Timp.	Tam Tam	BD	Timp.
Dan	SD	BD	Timp.	Cr. Cym.
Stephanie		Bells/Sus. Cym.	Xylo./Sus. Cym.	Bells
Jodi	BD	Chimes/Cr. Cym.	Cr. Cym./Sus. Cym.	SD

SELECTIVE BIBLIOGRAPHY

This selective bibliography attempts to group the list of available sources by the phase of score study (I, II, or III) utilized in the *Score & Rehearsal Preparation Worksheet*. In addition, after each listing below, you will find a series of numbers in parentheses (i.e. 1, 3, 6, 8, 11). These numerals correspond with numbered items on the *Worksheet* and indicate specific information that *may* be gleaned from that particular source. Please know that in some of the recommended texts, the information provided may only pertain to a few specific pieces of music.

This bibliography does not include full volume published biographies devoted to individual composers. Newly published or recently discovered sources may be found by consulting the garystith.blogspot.com website.

Phase I

Aldrich, Mark. *A Catalog of Folk Song Settings for Wind Band*. Galesville, MD: Meredith Music Publications, 2004. (3, 4, 6, 10, 11)

Ammer, Christine. *The A to Z of Foreign Musical Terms*. Boston, MA: ECS Publishing, 1989. (8)

Baker, Theodore. *Pocket-Manual of Musical Terms*. New York, NY: G. Schirmer, 1947. (8)

Battisti, Frank L. *On Becoming a Conductor*. Galesville, MD: Meredith Music Publications, 2007. (10, 14, 15, 17, 18, 21)

———. *The Winds of Change*. Galesville, MD: Meredith Music Publications, 2002. (1, 3, 7, 10, 11)

Battisti, Frank & Garofalo, Robert. *Guide to Score Study for the Wind Band Conductor*. Galesville, MD: Meredith Music Publication, 1990. (1, 2, 3, 4, 5, 7, 11, 12, 13, 14)

Burch-Pesses, Michael. *Canadian Band Music: A Qualitative Guide to Canadian Composers and Their Works for Band*. Galesville, MD: Meredith Music Publications, 2008. (1, 3, 4, 6, 11)

Chevallard, Carl. *Teaching Music Through Performing Marches*. Chicago, IL: GIA Publications, Inc., 2003. (1, 3, 4, 5, 6, 10, 11, 12, 13, 21)

Cipolla, Frank J. & Hunsberger, Donald. *The Wind Ensemble and its Repertoire*. Rochester, NY: University of Rochester Press, 1994. (3, 10, 11, 20)

Cirone, Anthony J. *Cirone's Pocket Dictionary of Foreign Musical Terms*. Galesville, MD: Meredith Music Publications, 2008. (8)

Fennell, Frederick. *A Conductor's Interpretive Analysis of Masterworks for Band*. Galesville, MD: Meredith Music Publications, 2008. (1, 3, 4, 5, 11, 12, 13, 20, 21)

———. *Basic Band Repertory*. Evanston, IL: The Instrumentalist Co., 1980. (1, 3, 5, 7, 11, 12, 21)

Garofalo, Robert J. *Chorale and Shaker Dance by John P. Zdechlik: A Teaching-Learning Unit.* Galesville, MD: Meredith Music Publications, 1999. (1, 3, 4, 6, 7, 8, 10, 11, 12, 13, 14, 20, 21)

———. *Guide to Band Masterworks, Vols. 1.* Galesville, MD: Meredith Music Publications, 1992 - 95. (1, 3, 4, 5, 6, 7, 8, 10, 11, 12, 13, 14, 20, 21)

———. *Instructional Designs for Middle/Junior High School Band.* Galesville, MD: Meredith Music Publications, 1995. (1, 3, 6, 8, 11)

———. *On A Hymnsong of Philip Bliss by David R. Holsinger: A Teaching-Learning Unit.* Galesville, MD: Meredith Music Publications, 2000. (1, 3, 4, 6, 7, 8, 10, 11, 12, 13, 14, 21)

———. *Suite Francaise by Darius Milhaud: A Teaching-Learning Unit.* Galesville, MD: Meredith Music Publications, 1998. (1, 3, 4, 6, 7, 8, 10, 11, 12, 13, 14, 20, 21)

———. *Wind Band/Ensemble Anthology: Folk Songs & Dances in Wind Band Classics, Vols. 1 – 5.* Silver Spring, MD: Whirlwind Music Publications, 2002-2005. (1, 10, 11)

Goldman, Richard Franko. *The Band's Music.* New York, NY: Pitman Publishing, 1938. (1, 11)

———. *The Wind Band, Its Literature and Technique.* Boston, MA: Allyn & Bacon, 1961. (1, 11, 17, 21)

Griggs, Carolyn Doub. *Music Translation Dictionary: An English, Czech, Danish, Dutch, French, German, Hungarian, Italian, Polish, Portuguese, Russian, Spanish, Swedish Vocabulary of Musical Terms.* Westport, CT: Greenwood Press, 1978. (8)

Kinder, Keith. *Best Music for Chorus and Winds.* Brooklyn, NY: Manhattan Beach Music, 2005. (1, 3, 4, 7, 11, 12, 13)

Littrell, David & Racin, Laura Racin. *Teaching Music Through Performance in Orchestra, Vols. 1 - 3.* Chicago: GIA Publications, Inc., 2001-03. (1, 3, 4, 5, 6, 10, 11, 12, 13, 21)

Miles, Richard. *Teaching Music through Performance in Band, Vols. 1 – 8.* Chicago, IL: GIA Publications, Inc., 1997 – 2011. (1, 3, 4, 5, 6, 10, 11, 12, 13, 14, 21)

———. *Teaching Music through Performance in Beginning Band, Vols. 1 – 2.* Chicago, IL: GIA Publications, Inc., 2001 - 2008 . (1, 3, 4, 5, 6, 10, 11, 12, 13, 21) Mitchell, Jon Ceander. *Ralph Vaughan Williams' Wind Works.* Galesville, MD: Meredith Music Publications, 2008. (1,3, 5, 7, 10, 11)

Neidig, Kenneth L. *Conductor's Anthology, Vols. I & II.* Northfield, IL: The Instrumentalist Company, 1993. (1, 3, 4, 5, 6, 7, 10, 11, 12, 13, 15, 20, 21)

———. *Performance Study Guides of Essential Works for Band.* Galesville, MD: Meredith Music Publications, 2009. (1, 3, 4, 6, 7, 10, 11, 12, 13, 14, 17, 21)

Nicholson, Chad. *Great Music for Wind Band: A Guide to the Top 100 Works in Grades IV, V, VI.* Galesville, MD: Meredith Music Publications, 2009. (3, 4, 6, 10, 19)

Norton/Grove Concise Encyclopedia of Music. NY: W. W. Norton & Company, Inc. 1988. (1)

Paul, Timothy A. & Phyllis M. *Winds and Hymns: Resource Guide to Hymns, Chorales and Spirituals in Selected Wind Band Literature.* Galesville, MD: Meredith Music Publications, 2009. (3, 4, 6, 11)

Randel, Don Michael. *The Harvard Dictionary of Music, fourth ed.* Cambridge, MA: The Belknap Press of Harvard University Press, 2003. (1)

Rapp, Willis M. *The Wind Band Masterworks of Holst, Vaughan Williams and Grainger.* Galesville, MD: Meredith Music Publications, 2005. (1, 3, 4, 10, 11, 12, 13, 14)

Rehrig, William H. *The Heritage Encyclopedia of Band Music, Vols. 1–3.* ed. by Paul E. Bierley. Westerville, OH: Integrity Press, 1991. Supplement, 1997. (1, 11)

Salzman, Timothy. *A Composer's Insight: Thoughts, Analysis and Commentary on Contemporary Masterpieces for Wind Band, Vols. I–V.* Galesville, MD: Meredith Music Publications, 2003 - 2011. (1, 3, 4, 7, 10, 11)

Smith, Norman E. *March Music Notes.* Chicago, IL: GIA Publications, Inc., 1986. (1, 3, 4, 6, 10, 11)

———. *Program Notes for Band.* Chicago, IL: GIA Publications, Inc., 2002. (1, 3, 4, 6, 11)

Stoneham, Marshall, Gillaspie, Jon A., & Clark, David Lindsey. *Wind Ensemble Sourcebook and Biographical Guide.* Westport, CT: Greenwood Press, 1997. (1, 11)

Taruskin, Richard. *Oxford History of Western Music.* New York & Oxford: Oxford University Press, 2009. (1)

Weingartner, Felix. *The Post-Beethoven Symphonists.* London: W. Reeves, 1907. (1, 11)

Winther, Rodney. *An Annotated Guide to Wind Chamber Music: For Six to Eighteen Players.* Miami, FL: Warner Brothers Publications, Inc., 2004. (1, 3, 4, 6, 7, 10, 11, 12)

Zaslaw, Neal. *Mozart's Symphonies: Context, Performance Practices, Reception.* New York & Oxford: Oxford University Press, 1991. (1, 3, 11)

Phase II

Bailey, Wayne. *Conducting: The Art of Communication.* New York & Oxford: Oxford University Press, 2009. (11, 12, 13, 14)

Knight, John W. *The Interpretive Wind Band Conductor.* Galesville, MD: Meredith Music Publications, 2007. (11)

Weingartner, Felix. *On the Performance of Beethoven's Symphonies*, Ithaca, NY: Cornell University Libraries, 1906. (11)

Phase III

Adey, Christopher. *Orchestral Performance: A Guide for Conductors and Players.* London & Boston: Faber and Faber, 1998. (17, 21)

Barra, Donald & Menuhin, Yehudi. *The Dynamic Performance: A Performer's Guide to Musical Expression and Interpretation.* Englewood Cliffs, NJ: Prentice-Hall, Inc., 1983. (21)

Boonshaft, Peter Loel. *Teaching Music with Passion.* Galesville, MD: Meredith Music Publications, 2002. (21)

———. *Teaching Music with Purpose.* Galesville, MD: Meredith Music Publications, 2006. (21)

———. *Teaching Music with Promise.* Galesville, MD: Meredith Music Publications, 2009. (21)

Casey, Joseph L. *Teaching Techniques and Insights for Instrumental Music Educators.* Chicago, IL: GIA Publications, Inc., 1993. (21)

Cirone, Anthony J. *On Musical Interpretation in Percussion Performance: A Study of Notation and Musicianship.* Galesville, MD: Meredith Music Publications, 2008. (18)

Colwell, Richard J. & Goolsby, Thomas W. *The Teaching of Instrumental Music* (3rd ed.). Upper Saddle River, NY: Prentice Hall, 2002. (17, 21)

Garofalo, Robert J. & Battisti, Frank L. *Lead and Inspire: A Guide to Expressive Conducting.* Silver Spring, MD: Whirlwind Music Publications, 2005. (21)

Girsberger, Russ. *Percussion Assignments for Band & Wind Ensemble, Vols. 1 & 2.* Galesville, MD: Meredith Music Publications, 2004. (18)

Green, Elizabeth A. H. *The Dynamic Orchestra: Principles of Orchestral Performance for Instrumentalists, Conductors, and Audiences.* Englewood Cliffs, NJ: Prentice-Hall, 1987. (21)

Hunsberger, Donald & Ernst, Roy E. *The Art of Conducting* (2nd ed.). New York: McGraw-Hill, Inc., 1992. (21)

Labuta, Joseph A. *Basic Conducting Techniques* (5th ed.). Upper Saddle River, New Jersey: Pearson/Prentice Hall, 2004. (21)

Lisk, Edward S. *Creative Director: Conductor, Teacher, Leader.* Galesville, MD: Meredith Music Publications, 2006. (21)

———. *The Creative Director: Alternative Rehearsal Techniques.* Galesville, MD: Meredith Music Publications, 1995. (11)

———. *The Creative Director: Intangibles of Musical Performance.* Galesville, MD: Meredith Music Publications, 1996. (11)

———. *The Musical Mind of the Creative Director.* Galesville, MD: Meredith Music Publications, 2010. (21)

McBeth, W. Francis. *Effective Performance of Band Music: Solutions to Specific Problems in the Performance of 20th Century Band Music.* San Antonio, TX: Southern Music Company, 1972. (21)

Pizer, Russell A. *How to Improve the High School Band Sound.* West Nyack, NY: Parker Publishing Company, 1976. (21) Topolewski, Timothy. *Errata Studies for the Wind Band Conductor, Vols. 1–5.* Montreal, Canada: Plein La Vue, 1990-2007. (20)

Whaley, Garwood, ed. *The Music Director's Cookbook.* Galesville, MD: Meredith Music Publications, 2005. (21)

Williamson, John E. *Rehearsing the Band.* Galesville, MD: Meredith Music Publications, 2008. (21)

Professional Journals

Bandworld (www.bandworld.org)

Bulletin of the Council for Research in Music Education (bcrme.press.illinois. edu)

CBDNA Journal (www.cbdna.org)

Journal of the Conductors Guild, 5300 Glenside Drive, Suite 2207, Richmond, VA 23228.

The Instrumentalist, 200 Northfield Road, Northfield, IL 60093.

The Journal of Band Research. William J. Moody, Editor, Music-University of South Carolina, Columbia, SC 29208.

Winds (The Journal of the British Association of Symphonic Bands and Wind Ensembles), Solway, Ffordd Siliwen, BANGOR, Gwynedd, LL57 2BS, UK.

WASBE Journal (Journal of World Association of Symphonic Bands and Ensembles), Verlag Hans Obermayer, Buchloe, Germany.

About the Author

Gary Stith is Professor and Coordinator of Music Education at the Greatbatch School of Music, Houghton College in Houghton, NY. From 2002–2010, he also served as Conductor and Music Director of the Houghton College Symphonic Winds. He holds degrees from The Ohio State University and the Eastman School of Music, as well as the Certificate of Advanced Study in Educational Administration from the State University College of New York at Buffalo. His conducting teachers have included Donald McGinnis, Frank L. Battisti, Charles Peltz, Arnold Gabriel and Frederick Fennell and he studied timpani and percussion with Cloyd Duff, John Beck, John Rowland, James L. Moore, William Youhass, and George Ward.

Stith taught instrumental music in the Holland and Williamsville (NY) Central Schools for a total of thirty years, also serving as Instructional Specialist for the Fine and Performing Arts in the Williamsville schools from 1993–2002. During his tenure in Williamsville, he founded the Williamsville Concert (Community) Band and established the national Williamsville Commissioning Consortium for the commissioning of new works for wind ensemble. Past President of both the New York State Band Directors Association and the New York State Council of Administrators of Music Education, he was the northeast regional recipient of the 1976 ASBDA–Stanbury Award, the Outstanding Educator Award at the 1993 World of Music Festival in Chicago, the 2003 Buffalo Philharmonic Orchestra/ECCMC Award for Excellence in Music Education, and the 2010–11 Houghton College Excellence in Teaching Award.

He has authored numerous articles and penned chapters for the *Conductors Anthology*, *The Drum and Percussion Cookbook*, and served as Consulting Editor for a compilation entitled *Classic Beginning Solos for the Complete Percussionist*.

He continues to serve on the conducting faculty at the Csehy Summer School of Music and remains active as a guest conductor, clinician, and adjudicator.

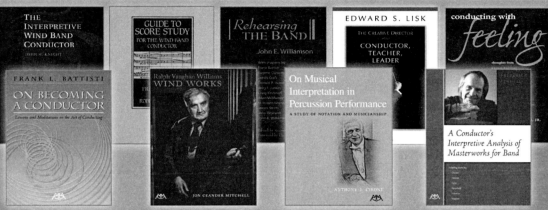